Lowe̶l̶l̶ ... ̶̶̶̶̶̶̶̶̶ ̶̶oma̶s̶

PAGEANT OF ROMANCE

Pageant of Romance

BY

LOWELL THOMAS

In collaboration with
FRANCES R. THOMAS

Autographed Edition

BOOKS, INC.
—
Distributed by
E. P. DUTTON & COMPANY, INC.
New York, 1943

TO

J. HOWARD PEW

President of the Sun Oil Company, which
sponsors the radio program in the compiling
of which so many of these stories were gathered.

Preface

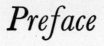

Books, magazine stories, stage plays and motion pictures in the vast majority concern sentimental romance. Fiction virtually equals love story. So we have ample opportunity to know how hearts throb on printed pages, the dramatic stage and the flicker screen. We derive from the imaginings of authors much of our idea of the diplomacies, negotiations and battles of the sexes.

Authors' inventions on the subject run in styles, conventions of the day. Some of the rough realism and unrealism of the present would hardly have been recognized as romance at all by an earlier generation that sighed over sugary gentilities and invariably happy endings. Fashions revert to the scandals of

PREFACE

Restoration comedy and the racy tale-telling of the Renaissance, back to Boccaccio. The Middle Ages exhibited the high-mannered mode of chivalry and mystical sentimentalities, as in Dante. And so back through the centuries to the Greeks, whose tragedy and comedy so often got along without any love interest whatever.

The fictional pageant of romance is there for all to read, but sentiment is lived, as well as imagined. So what about a pageant of the romances that flourish or wither in actual life? How about a review of love stories, such as are experienced by all sorts of people every day? This book is a compilation of just such factual happenings in the rose-strewn realm.

As a lifelong collector of stories, I could hardly have failed to gather a large sheaf of true tales with lovelorn themes. Traveling about the world in younger years, I conned episodes of adventure in such places as Alaska, Arabia, India, the Indies and the South Seas. I found that adventure thrill has frequently its turn of the boy-girl theme—boy-girl being a mature middle age often enough. I found, too, that even in the most adventurous haunts or hazard the prize story of the day might deal exclusively with those languishing emotions—minus tigers, crocodiles, gun shots and other violent appurtenances.

Later, reciting a nightly news program on the radio, I found that the tidings of the day were richly gingered with incidents and disturbances under the patronage of Venus. I have always tried, in my news program, to vary the weighty events, national and international, with a leaven simply human—and what could be more human than romance? I found the news to be a great purveyor of love stories, the ones that actually happen. These, as they appear on the press wires, are not developed with the elaboration of fiction, of course, but are swift with compressed drama and concentration on a point. That is how the current news gatherers, the reporters, pass along such raptures and brawls of passion as are interesting enough to put on the wires.

This Pageant of Romance presents love stories out of life. How alike are they to the imaginings of the fictioneers? You, yourself, can judge.

Contents

CONTENTS

PAGEANT OF ROMANCE

I

Triumph of Romance

The victories won by sweet sentiment, I find from my collection of stories, are of a rich variety. They are dominated, to be sure, by that favorite theme in the literature of sighs—the course of true love running roughly, only in the end to become as smooth as skates on ice. Tearful sadness may precede the bright consummation, or perhaps there may be a prelude of difficulties most rambunctious. The troubles may be for brief anguished days, or may be prolonged for years before the happy ending.

In life, unlike fiction, the course of true love is sometimes perfectly smooth from beginning to end without hitch or obstacle—and the story can be told in a breath. Or easy victory may be followed by a doleful hiatus—requiring reconciliation for a felicitous termination. Then there are odd curiosities in the triumph of romance, to make the variety complete.

At Garfield, New Jersey, a cheering crowd attended a Thanksgiving Day wedding. Three hundred people jammed into the office at the City Hall, where the mayor of Garfield united in holy wedlock a husky sailor and his bride. Why all the public enthusiasm? Romance, pathos, sweetness and a happy ending.

Josephine Phillips worked in a silk mill at Passaic, New Jersey. Then she lost her job—employees laid off. She went looking for another job—went to New York. No luck—she couldn't find one. The little money she had vanished in a few days. She had no place to go. She became a waif and a stray in New York. She slept in subway trains, and walked in Central Park. Day after day she became more and more downcast, hopeless—and hungry.

One night, as she walked disconsolately in Central Park, a sailor came strolling. He accosted the girl, spoke to her. In wartime there were many girls in New York whom a sailor or a soldier might stop and address. But the strolling mariner sensed that there was something unusual, something pitiful, about this girl. He asked her what she was doing. She was heart-hungry for someone to talk to, someone who would give her sympathy. She told him of ten long days and

16

nights, hungry and wretched, with no place to go. Thus the girl in the park related her story to Sailor Bill Langford of Victoria, Texas.

Sailor Bill took Josephine to a restaurant, and bought her a square meal. He offered to give her money to get a room for herself. She wouldn't take it. They spent the rest of the night sitting and talking until dawn. In the morning Sailor Bill had to go back to his ship. He told Josephine he would meet her at the same place in the park on the following night.

Josephine spent the rest of the day in the subway, catching a bit of sleep as she sat in a car. The day seemed terribly long. Wouldn't night ever come, the time for her date with Sailor Bill? It finally did—and to the park she went, keeping the date. She waited. No sign of Sailor Bill. Then a man approached and asked her if she was Josephine. He had a note for her. She read it, and her heart sank. By a bad break of luck and Navy Department orders, Sailor Bill's ship had put out to sea—and he was aboard.

That seemed to be the end of things for Josephine. All she could do was go on sleeping in subways and walking in the park, day after day, night after night. Finally she was picked up by the police and sent to the House of Detention as a vagrant.

Her story became known, and got into the newspapers as a human-interest heart throb. Aboard ship, at sea, Sailor Bill had not forgotten. He appealed to his Commander for leave to go to Josephine—he wanted to marry her. The publicity attracted the notice of a cousin of Josephine's out in New Jersey.

This cousin offered her a home until Sailor Bill could come and get her. So to Garfield, New Jersey, she went and waited—and not in vain.

The wedding occurred on Thanksgiving Day—what a day of thanks for Josephine! The whole town was waiting, so appealing was the story. A crush of people attended. There was half an hour of congratulations and handshaking before Josephine and Sailor Bill could get away. They started off on their honeymoon with enough money to set up housekeeping. A Hollywood producer paid them two hundred dollars for the movie rights of their love story. So it was a perfect Thanksgiving Day for the once homeless Josephine and her gallant Sailor Bill.

In Boston a wedding was solemnized at the fashionable Mount Vernon Congregational Church in the aristocratic Back Bay district—and a most formal wedding it was. Stately procession, bridesmaids and ushers, music, orange blossoms and a sumptuous wedding gown and veil—and then a wedding party with huge cake, a five-piece orchestra, and dancing. What prominent personalities of society were getting married? The groom was a private soldier—just an ordinary fellow in the ranks. And the bride? She was no millionaire heiress—just a girl marrying a soldier. But there was a story behind the paradox.

Private Wallace Bell and Aileen Koyonan didn't think they'd need a formal wedding. In fact, they didn't have the price of anything elaborate. A quiet trip to get hitched seemed sufficient. But then Aileen got a wedding present from her sister—and what a present!

Aileen's sister was a fashionable modiste in Hollywood, a creator of styles for the stars of filmland. So the present she sent to Aileen was a wedding gown and veil. The gown was of flowing white satin, with a lace bodice, streaming ribbons and a long train. The veil was of shimmering gossamer trimmed with orange blossoms. Any girl would dream of getting married in that. Aileen gazed with gasps of wonder—and then with a sigh of dismay.

She certainly couldn't wear that gorgeous creation on a mere trip to the preacher's house for a quick splicing and a speedy getaway. The gown required a wedding to match, a formal church ceremony. However, the fact remained that the young couple did not have the price of anything like that. So what could Aileen do? It looked as if she could hand that wedding dress on down to her granddaughters—the gown in which Grandma did not get married.

Then a good fairy stepped in, a good fairy in the guise of the Women's City Club of Boston. These ladies heard about the dilemma of Private Bell, Aileen and the wedding gown, and felt sentimental about it. Thereupon they decided to arrange a formal church ceremony for the soldier and his bride. So that is how Private Bell and Aileen got married at the fashionable Mount Vernon Congregational Church in the aristocratic Back Bay section of Boston—with as much social fanfare and flutter as if it were the wedding of a Cabot and a Lodge—and was Aileen queenly in that bridal gown and veil!

Over in North Africa, Lieutenant Bertram Froehly of the Air Corps and Lieutenant Elaine Bost, an Army nurse, got married. There was no use in trying to escape romance and matrimony any longer—the way luck and Army orders were breaking.

Bert Froehly and Elaine Bost went together down in Georgia, and then he was ordered to Britain with his outfit. They postponed their wedding indefinitely, until he got back. A little later Elaine, now in the Red Cross, was ordered to Britain. They met there, and courtship continued. It was discontinued when Lieutenant Froehly was ordered to North Africa.

He was flying and fighting in the Tunisian campaign when he heard that a shipload of nurses was due in port. He had a hunch. He met the boat at the dock, and, sure enough, as the nurses trooped down the gangplank, there she was—Elaine. I suppose they figured that they might as well get married—because Army orders were throwing them together all the time anyway.

The word of their wedding was received by the mother of the bridegroom together with further word that Flyer Froehly had been wounded in action. But he was recovering nicely—after getting all tangled up with the darts of Dan Cupid and the bullets of the enemy.

🦀

There was a sailor in the Navy who certainly should have been marked down as a great persuader. At Denver, Electrician James Culp fell in love with Bobbie Yowell, and they decided to get married. She, however, was under age, and her father's consent was necessary. That was difficult. It seemed most unlikely that Papa would say, "Bless you, my children."

Sailor Culp, however, went to Bobbie's father and started talking. He talked so eloquently, he not only got Papa's consent, but also persuaded Papa to join the Navy!

🦀

Here is a story to remind you of Little Red Riding Hood. Remember Little Red Riding Hood and the wolf? This account tells how a girl found a sure kind of protection against wolves. Of course, you might think that in this modern day, in a big city like New York, there would be little danger of wolves. However, here's the tale of wild animal life.

Barbara Britton is a starlet of motion pictures. She is blue-eyed and blond. Now, Barbara has a boy friend —in fact, more than that. He is her "best boy friend," says she. And he is in the Navy. Her new discovery is the wearing of a pin. It's in the shape of a heart, and she wears it over her heart. It's decorated with the letters "U.S.N." and an anchor, indicating that he is in the Navy, and that she is anchored to that best boy friend.

This is charmingly sentimental in point of love and romance—but, strangely, it also has to do with wild animals. It appears that wolves are discouraged by a heart, the faithful anchor and the insignia of the Navy —worn over a girl's heart. We must ask the professor of zoology about that.

Anyway, Barbara recommends her invention to other girls, and explains it in the following scientific terms: "The idea," says she, "is just to win the wolf's respect—so he won't get ideas." Now, what ideas would a wolf have? Something about pursuing a gentle doe? We'll have to ask the professor of animal psychology about that.

Barbara relates that during several days in New York she has been to the Statue of Liberty, to the top of the Empire State Building, through the subway— and she went to see the Dodgers play. And not a wolf has chased her—all because of the magic pin.

And that, my children, is more cheerful than the bedtime story of Little Red Riding Hood and her Grandma, who so sadly were eaten. The modern Red Riding Hood has not been devoured by a wolf—and neither has her Grandma.

A great kidnaping mystery came to a romantic ending. There was sensation in the news as it flashed across the wires—one of the biggest of manhunts was on in the Middle West. And why not? Harry Bennett was chief of personnel for Henry Ford, in charge of a hundred and forty thousand Ford workers. He was in command of the Ford Company private police, a formidable organization. As such he had been in bitter conflict with the C.I.O. union elements trying to organize Ford employees. Harry Bennett, moreover, had lent a hand in the breaking of many a crime case. There were many who might have harbored a grudge against him. This mighty magnifico lived in a mansion like a castle at Ypsilanti, Michigan. He had three daughters, one of whom was Gertrude, fondly called "Trudy."

Some while previously Harry Bennett, as chief of the Ford personnel, had given a job to a young man named Russell Hughes. A lively chap was Russell Hughes, known for his skill as a tap dancer and as a drummer in a jazz band. Thanks to the job which the Ford executive gave him, he saved enough money to go to college. He became acquainted with Trudy Bennett, and romance began to blossom. There was no indication that it had the parental approval.

The kidnaping sensation began early in the morning when Trudy Bennett and her sister Billy started off in their car—returning to college after the Christmas holidays. Their car was stalled—frozen brakes. So Trudy phoned Russell and he came hurrying in his car and drove the girls to school. Those frozen brakes brought romance to a climax.

Later in the day Trudy phoned Sister Billy, asking Billy to call for her that evening after dinner. At the appointed time Billy called at Trudy's college quarters —but no Trudy. She wasn't there, and nobody knew where she had gone. Billy informed her father, and he at once suspected foul play. As hours passed on and Trudy was still among the missing, he was certain she had been kidnaped.

"Trudy would call me, I am sure," he argued. "She has never failed me. If she's all right she would let me know."

So he was certain it must be kidnaping, and the manhunt was on—the local police far and wide, the mighty G-men and the Ford Company police taking part in the search.

To be sure, there were signs of an elopement. Trudy was reported to have been seen driving off with Russell Hughes. It was revealed that Russell himself had left home taking an extra pair of shoes and a suit of clothes. And a bank reported that Trudy had withdrawn fifty dollars from her savings account that day. But the anxious father refused to believe; he scouted any such idea as elopement.

Indignantly he said: "Trudy always did what she wanted, and told me to go to hell. But she never kept anything from me." He had faith in his daughter, and that's like any fond father. It could only be kidnaping.

So the manhunt was redoubled; the cops, the G-men and the Ford police got busier than ever, combing the country for miles, searching for the criminals.

There was one fine and touching thing when Harry Bennett received a telegram from Richard Franken-steen, the C.I.O. leader in charge of the union campaign to organize the Ford workers. He had been at bitter odds with the chief of the Ford personnel and police. But in this moment of fatherly anguish, all was forgotten. "On my own behalf, and for the other United Automobile Workers of America," the union chief telegraphed, "I want to express the sincere hope that Miss Bennett is found soon and unharmed. The union's relations with the Ford Company and with Harry Bennett himself have at times been less than cordial, but all of us unite in sympathy with him to-day." Noble words, generous and impulsive sympathy toward an enemy whose daughter had vanished.

It worked up to a climax in a big way, the climax being a dispatch from Auburn, Indiana. There Russell Hughes and Trudy Bennett took out a marriage license, and immediately got married. They departed for Toledo on their honeymoon. Why didn't Trudy phone father? Maybe she was scared.

Word was flashed to the grieving Bennett family in the castle at Ypsilanti. It was told at once to the anxious father. What relief, what joy! Trudy not kidnaped at all, just married. What parental words were heard? What exclamations? Here were the words of the father: "Let 'em come home when their money runs out."

So all ended happily, and the last thing heard was an echo such as has often accompanied the peal of wedding bells. Growled Harry Bennett, the father: "I hope the guy has a job and can support her!" What many a father has said down through the ages.

Billy Conn did not get married that day. The wedding failed to happen though all was ready at the church—St. Philomena's Catholic Church in Pittsburgh. A crowd of five thousand, largely boys, was gathered to get a glimpse of Billy the Battler, who so nearly snapped the crown from the dusky brow of champion Joe Louis. But the bridegroom and bride failed to show up.

Billy Conn stayed at home. There he told inquiring newspapermen that it might be some time before he would be wedded. He put it in these plaintive words: "I'd love to be married today—but I can't." It was a melancholy plight for the fist-fighting young Irishman, who so gaily peppered the tawny face of the Brown Bomber in a bout for the heavyweight title.

What happened? Why didn't the wedding occur according to schedule? The father of the prospective bride announced his violent opposition to the marriage. An ex-baseball player, he didn't want his daughter to wed a prizefighter—a subtle social distinction. Harsh words were spoken by the father on the other side of the fence. Papa Conn rose in Gaelic indignation because Papa Smith said something about punching Billy unless he stayed away from eighteen-year-old Mary Louise. To that Papa Conn responded thus: "Smith might lick Billy," he roared, "but I'll be darned if he can lick me. He ain't never punched a Conn, and it'll be a sorry day for him when he tries."

Later Billy did marry Mary Louise, and still later there was a kitchen argument in which Billy the boxer broke one fist on his father-in-law's head. The triumph of romance did not stop the brawling.

Word from the Coast told of a tale of romance—love victorious. It was sentiment gilded with millions, for the swain and suitor was the heir to a great fortune. He loved, oh, so fondly, and in the end the word was—wedding bells. This sweet news came from the District Attorney's office at Los Angeles. The D.A. seems an odd source of tidings about heart throbs and orange blossoms. But this romance had been an explosive one, with raiding and brawling, fist fights, police—and a half-million-dollar suit for damages.

The story began with a millionaire whose son fell in love with a divorcée. The millionaire father objected with such remonstrance that Junior hired a lady detective to investigate his loved one. It seems that the lady detective found everything very much okay, because the next thing you know she and the divorcée were acquainted, were friends. And presently the millionaire was rushing to the District Attorney's office with a complaint that the two women at the lady detective's apartment were holding his son—a love captive.

This led to a police raid on the apartment to rescue the love captive. And things began to happen. There were two versions, but both agreed that an exciting time was had by all.

One story related that the fight began with the lady

detective hitting a gentleman detective a poke on the nose. That quieted down, and the father was talking to the son—the millionaire and the love captive—when the hostilities flared again. Once more the gentleman detective got it—a poke on the nose. Another fellow of the raiding party had his finger bitten. Junior was thereupon carried out, and they were putting him into his father's automobile when the lady detective stuck her head out the window and called out to the rescued love captive, telling him to fight. She shouted that old college refrain: "Fight, fight, fight." Junior followed that good advice, and the battle was on again. They went to it in the paternal automobile, until finally Junior was smacked down—subdued.

That was one version. The lady detective gave an entirely different account. She claimed they grabbed her and hurled her like a projectile. She landed on the furniture, slam bang on top of the bureau. They poked a gun at her and terrified her granddaughter. Granddaughter had hysterics, as why wouldn't she—seeing Grandma tossed around. That was why the lady detective proceeded to sue the millionaire for five hundred thousand dollars—because she was hurled like a projectile.

The course of true love certainly didn't run smooth in that case. But it all ended in beams of moonlight and the perfume of roses. For the report came that the enamored couple and the irate father talked it over in the District Attorney's office, and love had its way, the millionaire father giving his blessing. So all were happy now—except Grandma. The lady detective was still sore and suing.

🐚

Death came to the Merchant of Death. Sir Basil Zaharoff, mystery man of armament and war, went to make peace with his Maker. Time and again the news had had occasion to sketch his career and personality, speculate about the secrets of the man and recite the story of his singular romance. This was the last time.

He was the world's supreme magnate of munitions, king of armament, number one merchant of death. They said that the personal fortune he left was the greatest ever accumulated by one man. How much it was, nobody really knew, except that it was counted in billions. He sat on the boards of directors of three hundred great corporations. He was reputed to have made a billion out of the first World War alone, as munitions salesman to the Allies.

That was his supreme era. The Kaiser's Germany put a price of a hundred thousand dollars on his head. The Allied governments honored him with two hundred and ninety-eight decorations. Clemenceau once said, "Zaharoff is the sixth power of Europe." Six world powers: Great Britain, France, Germany, Russia, Italy —and Zaharoff.

His death certificate showed the mystery man to have been born in 1850 in Turkey. That would make him eighty-six at the time of his demise. His parents, the story went, were Greeks who fled to the highlands of Anatolia during Turkish massacres in 1821. The future Croesus was rumored to have been a tourist guide in Constantinople during his youth. Zaharoff himself, in one of his rare statements, declared that he had been educated in London and Paris. The legend that surrounded the sales agent for Mars was completed by his story of sentimental romance.

Long years in the past he had fallen in love with a lady of the most aloof Spanish aristocracy, the Duchess of Marchena, and she with him. But she was married, the wife of a cousin of King Alfonso. Zaharoff, the international lord of armament, waited for her for thirty years, until she became a widow. He was seventy-seven when they were married in 1924. She was sixty and a grandmother. A year and a half after the marriage she died—the wife for whom he had waited so long.

After that he lived in retirement in Monte Carlo. People said he owned the great gambling casino, but he denied it. The hobby of his old age was cooking. He spent his idle hours in a magnificent kitchen compounding dishes fit for Lucullus. During his last couple of years the salesman for Mars was an invalid in a wheel chair. Finally a heart attack, and death came to the Merchant of Death. The only one at his bedside, save doctors and nurses, was his stepdaughter, the Princess of Bourbon—daughter of the wife for whom he had waited those many years.

This is a Rumanian love story, but not about King Carol. It tells of a man named Klopatsko. It seems that Klopatsko fell in love with a rich farmer's daughter. Her parents said, "Nay, nay, Klopatsko." And he, poor fellow, thought that death was preferable to life without love. So he got a gun and took a shot at the girl, and at himself. He missed both the girl and himself. The judge gave him three years in the local hoosegow.

When he had served the three years, Klopatsko learned that his beloved had married a man named Nornwak. That broke his heart completely. So he went to the home of the bride and bridegroom and set the house on fire. This time the judge gave him two years in prison.

He served that sentence, was released, and shortly afterward met his beloved on the street. He discovered that she had been left a widow. So Klopatsko proposed marriage then and there. She accepted, and after all the stormy love-making became Mrs. Klopatsko. So let the wedding bells ring out.

A curious tale came over the cables from England. The scene of the story was the small town of Holmfirth in the West Riding of Yorkshire. In the middle of a Saturday afternoon the vicar of the principal church was preparing his sermon. He was startled by the sound of a single mysterious peal from the bell of his church. He left his study and went to investigate.

In the church he saw a woman kneeling by the altar rail. A middle-aged man entered and stepped quietly to the woman's side, saying: "I am here." The couple shook hands somewhat awkwardly, then suddenly put their arms around each other and knelt by the altar rail.

This is the tale they told the vicar. Many years previously they had been married in that same church. After a while there was a rift, a break of discord. The husband did something which the wife felt she never could forgive. So the couple separated by mutual consent.

They did so with one definite understanding. If the man really wanted to be reconciled, he must be near the church each year at two o'clock on the afternoon of their wedding anniversary. If he heard a single stroke of the bell he would know that his wife was inside the church, ready to forgive. For ten years the man visited Holmfirth regularly on the anniversary, and was near the church at two o'clock in the afternoon. For nine years he waited in vain for the message from the bell. But the tenth year, when he'd almost given up hope, he heard the telltale stroke pealing from the church bell in the steeple.

🐑

Here's a sweet sentimental story of love and reconciliation. The heroine was an heiress to the Gould fortune, a granddaughter of the fabulous millionaire, Jay Gould. The romance was a union of West and East, the prairie and the big town.

In New York the Gould heiress told how she was reunited to her cowboy husband, and was going back to the ranch in Wyoming. No more bright lights of Broadway for her. And she was renouncing her hope of a stage career. She was just going out there to ride the purple sage, to be a Western wife to a bronco-riding husband, keeping house on the ranch for Slim and the other cowhands.

It all began when Anne Gould Meador, while on a stay in the Wyoming cow country, was wooed and won by Herman Elsbury, head cowboy on a dude ranch. He was a seventy-five-dollar-a-month ranch hand, and she was a Gould heiress, but you know how love evens up all things. They were married and lived on the ranch, but after a while the heiress began to long for the big city. She developed an ambition for a stage career. So she came to New York and after a while she filed a suit for divorce.

When this word reached the cowboy husband, he in his impetuous Western fashion instantly hopped a train for New York. There he sought out wifie and his pleading was direct and forthright—for he was a cowboy from the wide-open spaces. And so a reconciliation quickly followed.

The cow puncher's heiress bride related the story fondly as she lay in bed in a hospital. First of all, she denied that she got her broken shoulder when her husband tossed her down a flight of stairs. Oh, nothing like that! She explained that she fell off a horse and broke her shoulder. How come the reconciliation? She explained it by saying that she couldn't understand why she ever filed that divorce suit.

Standing by her hospital bedside, her cowboy hubby declared that Jay Gould's granddaughter had learned how to cook. She was great at baking banana cream pie. "There's a lot for her to do on the ranch," he explained. So he hoped she'd soon get over her broken shoulder.

To which the Gould heiress echoed with a sigh, "I'm just a ranch girl now—git along, little dogie."

The candles glowed and glittered just as brilliantly as had been expected. The wedding of the candlemaker's daughter was solemnized as resplendently as the newspapers had announced. Papa Ajello was the greatest candlemaker in the land, and his daughter, Virginia, was the light of his life—the wax candle of his life.

The King of Candles had made glowing tapers for kings, queens, and Presidents. The biggest he ever molded was a great Caruso memorial candle, which weighed one ton and was designed to burn one day a year, on All Saints' Day, for eighteen hundred years in the Church of the Madonna of Pompeii at Naples.

So when Papa Ajello's little Virginia was married the church in the Bronx was filled with the radiance of two hundred and ninety-eight great tapers—and with the perfume of candles. For each candle was scented, and as it burned it gave off a fragrance of orange blossoms or lilies of the valley. There was light mingled with perfume at the wedding.

❦

Mary Magdalene got married. Yes, Mary Magdalene of the Passion Play at Oberammergau. She was pretty Clara Mayr, twenty-five years old. The bridegroom was the son of Anton Lang, famous for his impersonation of the Savior. There was a celebration fit for the wedding of a king in the little Bavarian village of Oberammergau. For the actors in the Passion Play were the nobility of the town, and the family of Anton Lang the noblest of all. The young couple announced they were going to America, Mary Magdalene and her bridegroom. Young Anton Lang had been engaged to teach German in one of our universities.

❦

News that Charlie Chaplin was married came with a Chaplinesque twist—an impish turn of surprise. The bride was Charlie's co-star, Paulette Goddard. He was not yet fifty. She was somewhere around that incredible age of twenty. Actually they had been married for two years, but had kept it secret so that the bride might continue her movie career on her own merits and not as the wife of Charlie Chaplin.

The tidings emanated from neither the bridegroom nor the bride, but were disclosed at Hollywood by

Randolph Churchill, son of the Right Honorable Winston Churchill, now the wartime Prime Minister of Great Britain. That was a rather stately way of breaking the news to Hollywood. Randolph Churchill, who was a writer and lecturer, told how the news was broken to him. That also was rather odd.

It happened at teatime. Young Churchill, talking to Charlie Chaplin and Paulette Goddard, made some reference to an insistent rumor that they were engaged. They both denied it. They denied they were even thinking of it.

"It's ridiculous," said Charlie Chaplin. "We're not engaged—we're married and have been for some time."

That's how the marriage of Charlie Chaplin, Comedian Number One, was announced—with a comic twist.

Here is a love story that might be entitled, "From Cupid to Romeo." At Reno Mrs. Bertha M. Buckley was divorced from her husband. His name was Cupid Buckley. Immediately afterward she took out a license to marry Romeo Whitten. Marrying first Cupid and then Romeo would seem to be the height of romance—or the height of something.

From Hollywood came a headline both romantic and financial—kisses at fifty thousand dollars each. Patriotic too—because the kisses were accompanied by war bonds. The lady in the case was Lana Turner, one of Hollywood's most beautiful stars—also one of the most blonde.

When Lana started on her bond-selling tour, her studio provided her with some written speeches—sales talks. But they weren't Lana's kind of oratory. "They were swell speeches," she explained afterward, "all about friends, Romans and countrymen. I told the head men," she continued, "that I couldn't talk that kind of stuff." They responded, well, in that case she could say it with kisses, give a kiss to each buyer of fifty thousand dollars' worth of bonds.

"I said I thought it was kind of cheap," she related. They said, "Not at fifty thousand dollars per kiss, it wasn't cheap!" And Lana had to agree. "A kiss at fifty thousand dollars," she conceded, "is really very expensive. Believe me, it isn't worth it."

The truth of that remark would seem to be illustrated by what happened. "The first fifty-thousand-dollar customer," she said, "was—two nice old ladies. That was a jolt. But I took their money and kissed them both."

Another fifty-thousand-dollar customer was described by Miss Turner in the following words: "He was about eighty years old. He walked with a cane. But he had his fifty thousand dollars, and he wanted a kiss."

However, there was a break of luck for Lana. "Next," she exclaimed, "came a twenty-one-year-old boy." He, however, didn't have fifty thousand dollars. A twenty-one-year-old seldom has, as most girls know. He had only five thousand—which was sufficiently surprising. "I didn't see how such a young boy could have saved up five thousand dollars," mused Lana, "but there it was, so I gave him a kiss."

The newsreel men insisted that she do it all over again. So she gave the twenty-one-year-old two kisses. Consequently he got twice as much for five thousand as the others for fifty thousand, which would seem to indicate that there is some advantage in being twenty-one. Or maybe his patriotism was greater.

Anyway, the kiss-me-again, buy-a-bond tour was a great success. Lana Turner sold more than five million dollars' worth. I wonder what Helen of Troy or Cleopatra would think of that—five million dollars' worth of kisses?

A young woman entered the United States, and awaiting her in this land were twenty thousand dollars and three thousand proposals of marriage. Talk about American hospitality! We all know what we could do with twenty thousand bucks, but three thousand proposals of marriage might embarrass even the most romantic of us.

The lucky girl was Vera Hruba. Vera was a blonde from Czechoslovakia, a figure skater—with the accent on figure. And her face was all right too. She came to the United States, where her figure figured in a lot of figure skating. The only trouble was that her permit for staying in the country ran out. So the story broke that she'd have to go back to Nazi-dominated Czechoslovakia unless—unless she promptly procured an American husband. Marriage to an American would permit Vera to stay on.

In the publicity that attended her plight, Vera the figure skater described herself in these terms: "a romantic, home-loving girl." With a disposition like that, a husband wouldn't be so hard to take—and Vera was resigned to it. The publicity got a good response —three thousand gentlemen were willing to enable Vera the figure skater to remain in the good old U.S.A.

In the meantime Vera was informed that she could renew her stay in this land by going to Canada and re-entering under the Czechoslovakian immigration quota. So she went to Canada, and re-entered the United States. The proposals of marriage—a mountain of them—were waiting for her.

Moreover, at Lafayette, Indiana, Mrs. Nan Foley died and left Vera a legacy of twenty thousand dollars. We were not told just why. That and three thousand suitors—the luck of Vera the figure skater.

At Kansas City a man announced that he was not going to join the union. He was Raymond Carter, who had a little jewelry shop. It was a one-man affair. Ray was both employer and employee, both capital and labor, all by himself. He couldn't see much sense in joining the union. He might have to go on strike against himself, or sign a union contract with himself. But there was another reason, too.

Ray's shop was being picketed, and the union picket was a young lady, Miss Carol Harris. She paraded back and forth in front of Ray's jewelry shop, had been doing it for six months. Carol knew the beat so well that she read books while picketing. She perused four or five volumes a week pacing back and forth—thereby improving her education.

Ray, the non-union jeweler, enjoyed having his place picketed by Carol, the union girl. "It's a lot of fun having Carol around," Ray said. "She's a very sweet girl."

One time Carol's feet began to hurt from the daily march on the hard pavement. When Ray heard of this he spread a carpet out on the sidewalk for her to picket on. That made people laugh, and Carol didn't like the passers-by laughing at her. So Ray dutifully removed the carpet.

"The only thing she lets me do for her," said Ray, "is telephone the beauty parlor for appointments—and I'm always glad to do this." Quite right, Ray. If you're going to be picketed you might as well be picketed by a beauty.

Ray had to make a final decision about joining the union. He said, "No." If he did, Carol would stop picketing.

From Soviet Russia came word of a triumph of romance, and this expressed in one word, a sweet-scented word—perfume. In Moscow a perfume shop was opened—decidedly a novelty in the stern land of proletarian revolution. For years those terrifyingly serious people, the Bolsheviks, frowned on every vanity and frivolity of feminine loveliness. And when a Bolshevik frowned, vanities and frivolities vanished like a pretty dream when the alarm clock rings. So there was no powder, no rouge, no lipstick, no silk stockings.

Then at last the rules of Communistic Puritanism were relaxed. Feminine complexions blossomed, if not like the rose, at least à la drug store. Lips became as red as the red flag, and silk stockings were seen adorning the sturdy underpinnings of the feminine members of the Communist Party. The climax—a perfume shop! The Bolshevik beauties were made to smell as sweet as the rose gardens of Ispahan or the honeysuckle bowers of Alabama.

The Communistic perfumes had fancy names too, though not exactly like those tickling Parisian distillations. No such poetic perfumes as "Ecstasy of Love" or "Tonight or Never." One Soviet scent went in for romance so far as to be called "Red Divorce." But the others were given more revolutionary, political appellations, signifying sociology and the machine age.

One dreamy burst of fragrance was called "Five-Year Plan"; another, "Heroes of the Revolution." A third swooning concoction of the scent of violets had the chilly name of "Icebreaker"; while the most ecstatic of all, a voluptuous blend of tuberoses and lilies of the valley, was labeled "Five-Thousandth Tractor."

Those Marxian perfumes suggested a few ideas for modern poetry and passion. A rapturous lover might

41

say: "Olga, you have the lingering fragrance of the Five-Year Plan," or, "Darling, you smell like an ice-breaker back from six months in the Arctic." Or he might sigh: "Dearest, I seem to have in my arms the five-thousandth tractor!"

In Kansas a bus driver got tired of the way motorists ignored his signals when he thrust his hand out of the window, meaning "turn." They paid no attention to his hand. So out of wood he carved a leg, a beautiful leg, and put a silk stocking on it and a high-heeled shoe. Thereafter when he signaled "turn," he'd thrust that shapely leg out of the window, and did the motorists take notice!

At Long Beach, California, the oldest enlisted man in the Army reported back for duty—after a furlough. He came marching into camp with upright military bearing and a brisk step. Sergeant John Westervelt was seventy-three, and considered himself a number one patriarch among the troops of Uncle Sam. The Sarge at seventy-three returned from his honeymoon. He had just been married, and been given a honeymoon furlough. Some of the boys expected him to come in on crutches. But he marched in like an old campaigner. Nothing like military training, they say.

II

Thwarted Love

Time was when tragedy was the familiar accompaniment of romance—*vide* Shakespeare. Taste changed, and love stories seldom had endings other than happy. Life, however, is a great compromiser—midway between extremes. In the actualities of existence sentiment never was as luckless as in the former literature or as universally fortunate as in the subsequent optimism.

In the category of thwarted love we find tragedy somber and unrelieved, or the mournful may be touched with the ridiculous. Along with pathos simple and unqualified, we find parodies of heartbreak and grotesque uproars of romance—though the pang may be just as real for all the trappings of absurdity. There are deception and roguery, the betrayed girl or the trustful lover tricked by woman's wile. Varied indeed is the record of thwarted love.

Dark threads of tragedy were woven in the hapless end of two daughters of the American consul at the city of Naples. The two girls jumped from an airplane high in the sky, in circumstances of strange fatality and coincidence. Their double suicide recalled two other events that had occurred previously.

One of these was a great air disaster of the year— when a big British military plane, on its way from London to Singapore, crashed on the island of Sicily, and nine British officers aboard were killed. The two girls were close friends of two of the officers, attached to them by sentimental bonds—engaged to be married. Romance had begun when the British Army air transport had been detained in Naples for two or three weeks, and the party of officers had been regaled with social entertainments, merry parties. The two daughters of the American consul had fallen deeply in love. Then the great war bird had gone winging away to disaster.

In Naples the two girls heard the fatal news. They were plunged into grief, were haunted by the vision of the great sky ship smashing against the top of a Sicilian mountain—the swift, untimely end of the two men they loved.

Their parents sent them on a trip to distract their minds, a trip to England. You can reason it out for yourself, what passed between those two sisters, united in their common grief. In England they were seen weeping constantly. After a short stay, they took a plane bound for Paris. It appeared that they were returning home to their parents in Naples. The two girls were the only passengers aboard. Some time after the plane left London and while it was winging over France, the pilot noticed that his two passengers were missing and the door of the cabin was open.

Meanwhile, country people on the ground had observed the high winging plane, and had seen something fall from it, dropping the long way to the earth. This, in a strange and fantastic way, suggested to the French peasants the thought of gold. Everybody in those parts had heard much about a singular event of a week or so previously—when massive bars of gold had rained down to earth from a transport plane over northern France! Heavy ingots of yellow metal carried by the plane had bounced about and torn through the floor of the cabin. And the fall of treasure had caused a sensational gold hunt over the French countryside. Coincidence was at its most singular in this fact: the pilot of that extraordinary gold-dropping flight had been J. Kirton, and it was likewise he who was at the controls when the two girls leaped from the plane.

The French peasants on the ground found no shiny yellow metal. Instead, there were two bodies. They had fallen together, hands clasped, clinging to each other. The two girls in a suicide pact had leaped in each other's arms.

A strange and somber ritual was enacted at Colebrook, New Hampshire. One hardly knew what to think of it—not a wedding, yet a wedding ceremony, and it was a funeral. The bride stood beside a coffin, in which lay the body of her bridegroom.

They had been engaged—Clayton Bennett and Ida Knapp, and this was to have been their wedding day. But he had been killed in an automobile accident several days before. Ida Knapp, however, went through with the marriage ceremony at the appointed time. The ring was placed on her finger by the father of the man she would have wedded. And she placed a ring on the finger of her dead bridegroom. Then the funeral was held. Strange and somber indeed—a double ceremony of wedding and funeral.

In Minnesota, Michael Angelo Boncore suspected some fellow of stealing his money. Suspecting, Michael Angelo killed. He was tried and convicted and sentenced to a life term in prison. He served twenty-three years, and then at last the lifer was offered a pardon—on the condition that he return to the country he came from, Italy. Would he?

For all those prison years he had cherished a memory—the memory of a girl he had known when he was a young man in his native village. She had sworn eternal devotion, vowed that she would wait for him. As a life-term convict, Michael Angelo had given up all hope of gaining the girl of his prison dreams. He had not heard from her for years, but he was sure she was waiting. Now he was offered freedom, freedom if he would go back to Italy, back to his native village, back to the girl. He boarded ship rejoicing.

Months later Harry Walsh, a St. Paul lawyer who had been Michael Angelo's attorney, received a letter from him. The letter was postmarked Ethiopia. In it the one-time lifer told how he returned to the girl who vowed she'd be true, and found her long married with a large family of grown-up children. So Michael Angelo's prison dreams were shattered. In despair he went to an Italian recruiting station and enlisted for the Ethiopian war, eager for the miasmal fright of the tropics, bullets and bayonets, shot and shell—anything to forget!

In the country near Clayton, Missouri, people found a man chained like a dog. He was in a tent set up against a tree, had a dog collar around his neck, and was chained to the tree. The dog collar was padlocked, and the keyhole filled with cement—so it couldn't be opened. He had been there for four days— soaked by rain that had dripped in, and without a bite of food. It looked like some inhuman sort of crime, but the man chained like a dog explained—it was all because of love.

He was a local traveling scissors grinder, and he related that twelve years before he got religion and went to a camp meeting. There he saw a girl whom he described as his dream girl. "I met her in my dreams," he related—romantic dreams at a gospel camp meeting. He wrote to her, wrote to her time and again, but never got a reply. Then, after six years of scissors grinding and thwarted love, he mustered enough courage to ask the visionary damsel for a date. She went out with him once and then another time—and that was enough. She refused to see him. He could go right on grinding his scissors, so far as she was concerned.

He continued to implore his dream girl in prose and in verse. He wrote poems to her. He was too poetic apparently, for she had him arrested for annoying her, and he got thirty days in jail. That was a shock to the romantic scissors grinder. He brooded over it for a whole year, and then decided to chain himself to a tree. That was an odd manifestation of a broken heart, but he did it.

He picked a place within view of the dream girl's house, put up a pup tent, and chained himself like a dog. He didn't mind the lack of food. It was as he sighed to the sheriff: "I could go thirty or forty days without eating—since it was for love." His only complaint was that although his tent was within sight of the dream girl's house, she never bothered to look that way, didn't know he was in the tent, chained like a dog, and probably wouldn't have cared anyway.

He was certainly in the dog house, chain and all.

Paris was entranced by the "Romance of the Nose." Paris had decided opinions in the damage suit of the smeller. Indeed, messieurs and mesdames, Josephine the cook does deserve the damages. She has lost her sense of smell. The faculties of her nose have been dulled, if not obliterated. And how can Josephine be a cook without a good nose? How can she smell the sauce? How can she, without sniffing, detect the fragrant odor of the ragout and determine whether or not it is prepared in accordance with the art of the great chefs?

Josephine was one of the best cooks in Paris. The way she could prepare filet of sole Marguery was a treat to the gourmet. Her soufflé was a marvel to taste. Therefore it was a real tragedy when Josephine lost her sense of smell. How did she lose it? The answer is related in the form of a love story.

Josephine was stirring the sauce at the kitchen range, when monsieur, her employer, came into the kitchen. And what did he do? He tried to kiss Josephine. The story was not quite clear as to whether Josephine fell down because she resisted so hard or whether the mere enthusiasm of monsieur's kiss caused her to lose her footing. In any case, Josephine, the cook, fell and landed with her nose on the grate of the kitchen stove. That broke her nose.

Josephine was taken to a hospital, and there a plastic surgeon fixed her up. He restored her nose to its former pristine beauty. Her nose was as graceful as ever. But science tells us that noses are not merely to be gazed upon fondly and sentimentally—they are also intended for the function of smelling. And after Josephine's nose was reshaped she found she couldn't smell anything any more. Her nose didn't know the difference between madame's perfume and a slice of Camembert. And how could Josephine cook with a dull, dumb, insensitive nose like that?

So she went to court about it, and sued her employer for damages. The French judges considered the matter carefully. They remembered the importance of the nose to the human face and in the functions of human life. They remembered what the learned philosopher Pascal had said. "If," cried Pascal, "—if Cleopatra's nose had been a little shorter that might have altered the fate of the world."

The judges must have exclaimed: "Mais oui, if Cleopatra's nose was that important, how much more important is the nose of a cook!" So the Civil Tribunal in Paris awarded suitable damages to Josephine to recompense her for the lost sensibility, perceptiveness and wisdom of her nose.

We all have seen legal documents full of thorny, crabbed phrases of the law, but sometimes a paper drawn up by a lawyer can flash with something richly human. Take one passage from a complaint filed at Dallas, Texas. Many a man will recognize the style and tone, and reflect upon the wiles of woman.

A Texas oil man was suing a young woman to get back twenty thousand dollars' worth of gifts he had presented to her. They had been through the usual Great Romance, with an unusual amount of gives and takes, however—he giving and she taking. She was to have married the Texas oil man, but having received the presents she changed her mind and wedded a Chicago oil man. The lady must have had a fondness for petroleum, or at least a warm appreciation of things that petroleum money could buy—such as diamond bracelets, strings of pearls, emerald clips and a forty-five-hundred-dollar engagement ring. These were enumerated in court.

In the legal document the Texas oil man enumerated likewise a few things that the young lady had told him. She said that "he was a genius, a fine dancer and his company was superbly entertaining with never a dull moment, and he kept her in the clouds all the time."

Ever heard anything like that, fellows, words spoken so softly and with such feeling? I bet a lot of you have, though maybe you did not put up any twenty thousand dollars' worth of jewels and furs to hear it. Anyhow, that was what the girl said to the Texas oil man, whereupon she married the Chicago oil man. In other words, she was giving him the oil.

The blissful theme of marriage, of hearts united at the altar, was headlined in the stately realm of society and the Social Register, among the bluebloods and the élite. The bride was Mrs. Nan Pierson Brooks Macy Brill of the New York social set, daughter of a steel executive. She appealed to the police—wouldn't they please find her bridegroom? She had been married several days before to William Hunsaker Brill, wealthy sportsman. The next morning he went out, and she hadn't seen him since.

"I hope it's funny to somebody," said Mrs. Nan Pierson Brooks Macy Brill, "but it's not funny to me."

They had been married at Yuma, Arizona, married in a hurry and a rush. They had so little time to spare, that the wedding ring was from the Five-and-Ten. It cost a dime. The next morning the wealthy sportsman replaced it with something more appropriate to their social rank and riches. He left right afterward.

"I haven't seen Bill in person since," related the bride, "but he keeps telephoning, apologizing for breaking our appointments—saying he loves me very much indeed." Absence makes the heart grow fonder.

The police got busy, and found the bridegroom. He had gone on a party and had been on it ever since.

🌑

We know that love is fickle, romance fades quickly, and heart's devotion is easily obliterated. Tattooing, however, is altogether different. The marks of tattooing are not fickle, they do not vanish quickly, nor are they easily obliterated. This was amply proven in a Brooklyn story of a girl who was being treated for acid burns on one arm.

Mary Nuseld met a fellow named Jimmy. That was in the summer. Mary and Jimmy went down to Coney Island. The moon was shining, and everything was wondrous. They told each other their love was eternal, as eternal as something tattooed on your arm. Just to prove it, they went to a tattooing shop. The expert got busy with the needle, and tattooed a heart on the left arm of each.

Summer vanished, and so did Jimmy's love. His affection grew pale, but not the heart on Mary's arm. It stayed just as vivid and brilliant as ever. The climax came when Jimmy married another girl, and there on Mary's arm was that tattooed heart to remind her all the time of Jimmy's faithlessness in love.

The constant reminder was so painful that Mary set out to remove the tattooed heart. But that was painful, too. For, as I have remarked, tattooing is a lot more faithful than love. Mary procured some acid and tried to wipe the heart off with the burning liquid. She went about it too enthusiastically, and the next thing you know she was in the hospital being treated for acid burns.

Her injury was said to be painful, but not serious, which, I suppose, is a good description of broken hearts and things like that.

Kansas City was regaled by a suit for breach of promise of marriage. The defendant was a small-town banker. The lady, described as exceedingly shapely, had been his cashier.

In court she declared that they had been friends for seventeen years. Early in their acquaintance Banker

Sawyer's wife divorced him, and he thereupon proposed marriage to his pulchritudinous cashier. She accepted, but nothing happened. It took her thirteen years to come to the conclusion that Banker Sawyer did not really intend to marry her. She said that when she remonstrated he took her by the hand and told her she had a beautiful character. In fact, he intimated that it was too beautiful for marriage. He explained, moreover, that his first wife used to hit him over the head every morning. She, apparently, had a character just beautiful enough for marriage.

There was a moment in that trial which recalled a chapter from *Pickwick Papers,* the breach of promise trial of Bardell *versus* Pickwick, perhaps the most famous lawsuit in English literature. In one memorable passage Mr. Sergeant Buzfuz exclaims lyrically: "Chops and tomato sauce." At Kansas City it wasn't "chops and tomato sauce," it was "champagne and lobster." The complaining lady testified that she had champagne and lobster for thirteen years, but no wedding bells. Therefore she asked for a hundred thousand dollars—enough to provide champagne and lobsters for a lifetime.

The story of Zaro the aged Turk turned into a tale of broken hearts. Zaro Agah, one hundred and sixty years old and supposed to be the oldest man in the world, fell in love, was turned down, and died of a broken heart—so they said. But his was not the only one to be broken. When Amfe Amet Mutafa, a woman one hundred and twenty years old, heard of Zaro's death, it was such a shock that she, too, passed along to the Gardens of Paradise.

They were not exactly childhood sweethearts. Zaro had proposed to her a century before—when he was sixty and she was twenty. Her father said, "No!" Romance was sundered. But she never forgot him. For a hundred years she cherished the memory of that blissful time.

The story of the aged Turk had a large juicy element of improbability about it all along, and it certainly did rise to a high climax of improbability with the finale of broken hearts.

In the game of romance you should say it with wedding bells, not fire bells. Love may be alarming to some, but it shouldn't be a false alarm. All of these rules of the heart were violated by a young man of Montreal, who wound up in jail.

The story told how René Jobin was deeply devoted, but the girl's parents were cruel. They wouldn't let her see René. One night the mournful suitor was pacing disconsolately in front of his loved one's house, yearning for a way to meet her. Then he noticed in front of the house a fire alarm. And that inspired him to a flaming idea—only there were no flames. He thought, if you were to ring the alarm the fire engines would come thundering and clanging. In the commotion, the people of the house would rush out—parents, daughter and all. And he would have a chance to sneak her off to one side and be with her for a few minutes.

He tried it, and it worked. There was a fire alarm all over the place. The engines arrived with a roar. Papa and Mama came tearing down the front stoop, and daughter followed them. While Papa and Mama joined the firemen, looking frantically for the fire, René and his beloved had a blissful few minutes, exchanging vows of eternal devotion.

It worked that time. And it worked the next time. In fact, it worked eight times. Love was singing its own sweet song—and the Montreal Fire Department was driven crazy, not to mention the incessant agitation of Papa and Mama. But the ninth time—that was different! The Fire Department had cruelly set a watch, and they caught René ringing the false alarm. So René was in the soup, and presently in the coop —with the lovelorn girl hoping that by the time he got out he wouldn't be too old to marry her.

When a girl turns a fellow down, it's a painful experience—for the fellow. When six ambulances call for the girl, it sounds as if something painful might have happened to her. In fact, it was painful for several people.

A young lady of Manhattan had a persistent suitor. At home he would press his suit and then he would go to her house and press his suit. It didn't do any good.

The lady didn't respond to the suit pressing. The climax came when he called her on the phone and was told she was out. He called four or five times, with the same result. In fact, she *was* out. She was at a movie. He didn't believe it, and thought she was merely evading the suit pressing. It made him mad, so he proceeded to say it with ambulances.

One ambulance came clanking to her door and the interne said he had been called to take away the young lady suffering from a spinal injury. (That suit presser had a sense of humor!) A second ambulance arrived calling for the same lady. This time she was said to have a fractured skull. Six ambulances in all showed up, each attributing to her a different injury. The ailments were an interesting assortment. They seemed to symbolize the wishes of the suit presser. After the fair lady had decided there were too many ambulances attributing too many maladies to her, she called the cops.

In North Carolina, capital punishment is inflicted by means of the lethal gas chamber. That was the thought which horrified Lula Belle, the daughter of the town jailer at Lexington. In a cell of her father's jail were two young desperadoes, James Godwin and William Wilson. Godwin was charged with first-degree burglary, and if convicted, might be sentenced to the lethal gas chamber. North Carolina law made possible the extreme penalty for repeated criminal offenses. Actually, there was little likelihood of a death sentence for the burglar, but he made Lula think there was—he would have to die in the lethal fumes. Lula Belle, eighteen years old, blonde and sympathetic, thought of this with terror. Godwin was so young and personable.

The result of the sighing sentiment of the jailer's daughter was startling. In the absence of her father, Lula Belle took her father's key to the cells and also her father's pistol, and gave them to Godwin and his cellmate, Wilson. Whereupon they escaped. When Pappy returned and discovered what had happened, he locked Lula Belle up—in the same cell the robbers had occupied.

She confessed and added simply: "I just couldn't stand the thought of Godwin going to the gas chamber." To this she added one other thing that resounded with bitter irony. "He promised me faithfully," she wailed, "that he wouldn't get into any more trouble."

How the promise was kept was the subject of a flock of news reports. The police attributed to the pair a veritable crime wave that broke out—crimes of desperate escape, hold-up and murder. The fugitive outlaws, trying to steal an automobile, killed a man. Whereupon they did face the probability of the lethal chamber when caught—all because of the kind-hearted Lula Belle, the jailer's daughter, who in her sympathetic pity turned loose a crime wave.

When she faced the court to answer for her part in the jail break the testimony developed a mournful story of first romance. She was a big, husky, hundred-and-seventy-five-pound girl, and her father told how she could handle women prisoners like sacks of pota-toes—Lula Belle was that strong. However, her hefty strength was not so apt to make the boys sigh—not like the fragile wiles of the clinging vine. So it was some-thing new, it was first romance for Lula Belle, when soft words were spoken to her by the young prisoner in her father's jail, artful Robber James Godwin.

He told her he had got religion, and would be a good boy ever afterward. He repented the mistake he had made, and didn't want to be put to death in the lethal gas chamber. Lula Belle sighed, and turned loose the crime wave.

A jail in Iowa received a new convict —"a pure, hard-working girl." It seemed odd that in a state like Bible-reading Iowa they should send a virtuous and industrious maiden to the hoosegow. However, the pure, hard-working girl was a forty-two-year-old farmer—whiskers and all. The old rogue!

At the town of Mt. Etna, named after a volcano, lived Farmer Justain Butman, who had quite a vol-canic idea, a neat little gyp game. His scheme was to get in touch with matrimonial agencies by letter, and represent himself as a young woman desiring mar-riage. In that way he procured the names of various prospective husbands who had likewise approached the matrimonial agency on the subject of wedding

bells. To these Farmer Butman wrote shyly sentimental letters, always describing himself in those
touching words—"a pure, hard-working girl." He
stressed the purity part of it—the old rogue.

The lovelorn correspondence with a mail-order
suitor invariably developed into a proposal of marriage and a coy acceptance. Farmer Butman in accept-
ing always asked for carfare—railroad transportation.
What prospective husband would be so flinty-hearted
and stingy as to expect a pure, hard-working girl to
pay her carfare to her own wedding? So from fourteen
separate and distinct fiancés Farmer Butman collected
a total of eighty-four dollars.

In fourteen out of the fifteen times the scheme
worked without a hitch—matrimonial or otherwise.
Of course, the pure, hard-working girl failed to show
up for the weddings. It would hardly have done for
Farmer Butman to have appeared—whiskers and all.
So prospective bridegrooms were sadly disappointed,
but they took it on the chin with resignation, charging
it off to experience, blaming it on the perfidy of
women. Farmer Butman was adding to the already
dubious and historic reputation enjoyed by lovely
women.

In the last of these love affairs, however, something
went amiss. It was all because of the heart-throbbing
sentiment of a prospective bridegroom who was too
much in love. He sent ten dollars to bring his bride
to Portage, Wisconsin. Then he grew so eager for
the pure, hard-working girl that he couldn't wait. He
hopped a train and hurried to Mt. Etna, Iowa, to take

her fondly in his arms. And whom did he find? Instead of an innocent, blushing bride, it was Farmer Butman, the old rogue, stroking his beard.

You can imagine the situation. There was a painful scene, as a result of which Farmer Butman was locked up—and sentenced to six months in jail. So that was how in Iowa the prison doors closed on that pure, hard-working girl.

In New York, Marian Cribbs, a registered nurse, was sound asleep in bed. She awakened suddenly with an impulse to scratch her foot—it tickled. When she opened her eyes she saw at the foot of the bed a young man tickling her foot to awaken her. He quickly explained. "The reason I am waking you up," said he, "is that I am robbing you."

Marian Cribbs was a bright lass, and she started to talk her way out of trouble. She told the burglar she was a poor girl, just a nurse, and didn't have much that anybody would want to steal. The burglar replied that he liked to rob the rich, not the poor—something like Robin Hood. They had a long conversation about that.

Then Marian Cribbs suggested modestly that it was all a bit unconventional, she in her nightgown. She told the burglar she was sure that he wouldn't want to put his own sister in a position so embarrassing. He admitted that she was right, but before he left he had one thing to say.

"You are very pretty," sighed the burglar, "and I think I'd even like to marry you." He informed her that he had a thousand dollars saved up out of the proceeds of his burglaries, and concluded: "I'm sure we could make a go of it."

Marian Cribbs was exceedingly demure. She said it was all so sudden and really it wasn't the time and place for a proposal of marriage. She said that she'd consider it if he would telephone her for a date in the proper way.

He said he would—and did.

He phoned her. She made the date, and kept it—in the company of a detective. Then in jail the sighing burglar had leisure to meditate on the wiles of women.

In Los Angeles the police arrested a twenty-one-year-old burglar who committed his robberies with the strangest kind of weapon—a spray of perfume. Breaking into houses and stealing jewelry, he carried no pistol or anything like that—nothing but an atomizer for spraying the scent of roses and lilac.

Confessing to the police, he told the story of how he set out to be a gentleman burglar with a new idea. He thought up an original scheme for fooling the police, throwing the detectives off the trail. Committing a robbery, he'd make it appear to have been the doing of a woman—a lady burglar. That would fool the cops. He'd leave behind him a feminine trail— perfume. When he robbed a house, he'd spray perfume all over the place. So when Sherlock Holmes arrived he'd sniff sagaciously and mutter, "Ah, ha! A woman!"

The fragrant burglar was caught, but not because the trick of perfuming the larceny failed to work. His downfall came because he couldn't refrain from showing off before the girls. He tried to dazzle them with a display of the diamonds he had stolen. He gave them jewelry too—but only the least expensive pieces, the junk. They gaped at the real sparklers in vain. Maybe that's why they turned him in. For turn him in they did, informing the cops about the strange amount of jewelry in his possession.

He was right about the perfume, but he was wrong about women.

Near Taylor, Arizona, a mail truck was speeding along the road. Ahead was a passenger car, a sedan, which swerved and swung across the highway. The mail truck had to stop. Out of the sedan jumped two men with masks across their faces and pistols in their hands. They seized a twenty-two-thousand, five-hundred-dollar payroll, leaped back into their car and drove away.

A week later one of the two bandits, under arrest, told the police a strange story of crime adventure. He said that, having successfully committed the mail robbery, he and his outlaw pal decided how they'd invest the money. They'd tour the gambling houses of the nation, have a fling everywhere at the forbidden temples of chance. So they went on a magnificent journey of roulette and baccarat, poker and dice—everything. They proceeded from city to city, from gambling house to gambling house. This took them at last to Kansas City, and there they met their disaster, their Waterloo. Not at the roulette wheel or the poker table, however—but Waterloo in the guise of a pretty girl. Romance was their downfall.

They met a cutie in Kansas City and introduced themselves as gamblers from Seattle. After a pleasing acquaintance, she phoned them one day and asked them to meet her. They took a taxi to the address. There, two men stepped up to the cab, and pointed guns. It was a stick-up—robbers being robbed. They were relieved of some thirteen hundred dollars. This was all they had left of the twenty-two thousand five hundred dollars they had acquired in the mail-truck hold-up. The gambling had not been so lucky. And now the rest of it went, thanks to the cutie who had seemed to be such a pal.

That wasn't the worst of it. The taxi driver, burning with indignation, said, "We'll notify the police right away."

The one thing the two mail-truck burglars didn't want was anything to do with the police. They said: "No, what's the use of notifying the cops?"

The taxi driver insisted, and they realized that it was highly suspicious for robbery victims just to let it go at that. So they had to accompany the taxi driver to the police station and there they reported the robbery, keeping up the pretense that they were gamblers from Seattle. But the cops were suspicious, and held them for investigation. The one thing their story couldn't stand was investigation. So the truth was out —how the two mail robbers went on a gambling tour of the nation, and met a girl.

In Los Angeles, Charles Nicol was a professional magician. For years he entertained audiences with sleight of hand, one of his cleverest tricks being to show you how deftly he could pick your pockets. Magician Charles Nicol, as a part of the entertaining witchcraft, picked thousands of pockets.

He was not so good, however, at finding things— like finding a dog. One evening he was approached by a lady in distress, an attractive brunette. She had lost her dog. Would the kind gentleman help her find it? She was so pretty that the kind gentleman would indeed help her. They went looking for the dog—but all in vain. They never did find Fido.

The anticlimax came when later on the sorcerer found that his wallet was missing. The attractive brunette had picked the pockets of the magician pocket-picker.

Out in India the American consular authorities were interested in the case of a child bride who was an American citizen. The story came to light in a divorce action in southern India—a rich elderly merchant going to court and asking for an annulment of his marriage to a girl of thirteen.

The girl, Jasoda by name, was born in New York City of Hindu parents. They died, and she was taken back to India and placed in charge of guardians. These tried to find a husband for her, but it was difficult. Not because of her thirteen years, which made her no more than an ideal child bride. The difficulty was caste. The girl was of the highest caste, a Brahmin, and there were not so many prospective husbands in India who belonged to that God-like, twice-born division of humanity. Jasoda's guardians consulted a marriage broker, so anxious were they to procure a husband for the girl. The marriage broker was a tricky fellow and he talked the guardians into a cunning scheme.

At Jalgaon, in southern India, was a merchant named Nandlal. He was rich. He was old. He already had two wives but wanted a third. He was of the Vaisya caste, and this was two degrees lower than the lordly Brahmin. It is against the ancient law of the Shastra for people of different castes to marry, and Nandlal wanted a wife of his own Vaisya kind. The marriage broker went to him and told him of the thirteen-year-old Jasoda. He didn't say she was a Brahmin; he told Nandlal that Jasoda was of the Vaisya caste.

Nandlal saw the child. She was a comely maiden. He was well pleased. He paid a handsome fee to the marriage broker and gave splendid gifts to the girl's guardians. The wedding was celebrated in magnificent style. The girl went to live with her old husband and his two other wives.

Then Nandlal learned of the deception. He found that Jasoda was a Brahmin, of a higher caste than his own. He trembled with the knowledge that he had violated the ancient law of his Shastra. He acted immediately. He appealed to the local courts, asking that his marriage to Jasoda be annulled.

The judgment of the court was duly announced. It annulled the marriage. Nandlal was highly commended for his obedience to the Shastra in refusing to take a wife whose caste was above his own. The child bride from New York, who was an American citizen, was thereby divorced, but the court considered the fact that Nandlal was a rich man and that the girl didn't know that she had been misrepresented as a member of a lower caste. The judge therefore ordered Nandlal to pay her seven hundred dollars in gold. He was required also to give two hundred dollars to a benevolent society in the care of which the divorced child bride was placed.

The incident caused wide discussion in India—another example of the fidelity of the Hindus to their ancient laws, when a rich merchant divorced his child bride because her social rank was above his own.

🌿

In a courtroom at Paterson, New Jersey, a forty-five-year-old bachelor was saved from the fate of becoming a husband without being married. He protested earnestly, strenuously—no, he was not the lady's husband! But the lady insisted that he was. She also charged him with stealing a bankroll of money from her when he deserted her.

The story went back to 1922, eighteen years before, when the married life of Mrs. Benjamin Klein suddenly came to an end. Her husband deserted her and their three children, and furthermore decamped with all the money she had—all her savings. Eighteen years went by, and then one day Mrs. Klein, a resident of Paterson, New Jersey, was in New York—riding on an East Side subway. Suddenly she spotted a man entering the car and exclaimed, "There he is!"

She recognized him as the long missing Mr. Klein because of what she called his "identical appearance." This included an old scar on the upper lip. Also the same walk, the same mannerisms. The vanished Klein had been a pushcart peddler, and before that a silk dyer. The man that Mrs. Klein identified was also a pushcart peddler, previous to which he had likewise been connected with silk. He maintained, however, that he had been not a silk dyer but a silk weaver.

He utterly denied that he was Mrs. Klein's husband. His name was not Klein, it was Pigula, Leo Pigula. In 1922, when Mrs. Klein was deserted, Pigula was in Poland—so he claimed. None of this denial made any impression on Mrs. Klein. She had Pigula arrested on charges of desertion and larceny.

When the case came up in court, the outlook for Pigula seemed blacker than ever when testimony was given by Mrs. Sadie Kraus. She was a sister of Mrs.

Klein. Mrs. Kraus declared herself in these words: "I swear by all that is holy, that he is the man. I never saw such a resemblance."

The magistrate, Judge Rabinowitz, summoned all the wisdom of Solomon. He suggested that Mrs. Klein and Pigula have a talk together, and see if they couldn't straighten matters out. So the two went to one side and conversed. There was no quotation of what Pigula said to Mrs. Klein, but it was effective. After some minutes of conversation, the lady told the judge: "No, this is not my Benjamin." She admitted she had made a mistake.

Mrs. Klein then turned to Pigula. "I am sorry," she said, "that I have caused you so much trouble."

To which Pigula responded, "Get away from me."

This was a little ungallant, not exactly chivalrous, but no doubt it expressed Pigula's sentiments quite accurately—"Get away from me."

It's a terrible thing not to be able to speak English, so said Marcus Siris, a Greek. Marcus knew, because he was innocent of any knowledge of English. Up before the judge, he related a pathetic story, a tragedy of language.

At Ambridge, Pennsylvania, Marcus met Alexandra, and found her company delightful—because Alexandra, too, was Greek and spoke the Hellenic tongue, as well as English. One day she took him to the office of an American gentleman. Marcus didn't know it was a justice of the peace. Alexandra spoke in English, and Marcus didn't know what she was saying. The justice of the peace spoke, also in English—and Marcus didn't understand a word. Alexandra told Marcus to say an English word or two, like "Yes" and "I do." And Marcus mumbled obediently, not knowing what it meant. He was being married, but he didn't know it.

After a while he didn't go around with Alexandra any more, quite forgot her, until he was arrested for desertion and non-support. That's when he found out he was married.

In court Alexandra admitted that the story Marcus told had certain points of accuracy. She conceded that it might be that Marcus didn't completely understand that he was getting married, didn't quite fathom the meaning of the words when he mumbled "Yes" and "I do." He had acquired a wife, and it was English to him.

III

O, Beware, My Lord, of Jealousy!

There are some figures of speech so well established that, even if you avoid using them, the omission will be noted. They still are there—*in absentia*. So why pretend? Jealousy is the green-eyed monster—and we find the critter roaming and snorting everywhere, preying on the rich and the poor, the ignorant and the learned, the young and the old. The following incidents from lovelorn human life will hint at the scope of the green-eyed monster pursuing his adventures.

❦

The courtroom on the Arctic shore of Coronation Gulf was in a shack. Yet the court assembled with all the impressive dignity of British jurisprudence. His Majesty's justices had journeyed to the Far Northern coast by the sky route, by what the Eskimos call the "devil bird." The defendant was Ahigiak, accused of murder. The Canadian Mounted Police had brought him to Coronation Gulf from his own country, twenty sleeps by dog sled to the east. Witnesses told how Ahigiak had killed his friend, Anarauk.

They had been boys together and brother hunters in the chase of seal and caribou. They lived in the same ice hut with their wives and children. They were friends until one night in the winter of 1931. That night Anarauk took Ahigiak's wife. In the North there is no romantic courtship. Ahigiak's wife that night got up and went to Anarauk's side of the igloo.

On the witness stand Agnelliak, widow of frivolous Anarauk, told how that night Anarauk had emptied her out of the sleeping bag and Ahigiak's wife had crawled in. Every night for six months thereafter Ahigiak's wife went from Ahigiak's side of the igloo to Anarauk's.

Minniak, a young Eskimo, told how one day he had seen the wronged husband, Ahigiak, pick up a gun. Anarauk appeared. Ahigiak shot him in the back, and when he turned, shot him through the head. Two years later the Mounted Police, with Minniak as their guide, found Anarauk's bones scattered by the wolverines.

Ahigiak, the defendant, listened with amazement when his counsel pleaded "not guilty" for him. "It's not so," Ahigiak told the court. "I kill Anarauk. He had my wife. I kill him."

His counsel made a plea of the unwritten law. The

72

jury brought in a verdict of manslaughter. When the word manslaughter was translated into Eskimo, Ahigiak smiled and nodded. "That is right," he said. He sat silent and unmoved when the judge sentenced him to serve five years in the nearest jail—at the outpost of Aklavik, eight hundred miles to the west.

The death of Kid McCoy by his own hand was the occasion of many a reminiscence of pugilism and of the Kid's flagrant vagaries of romance. He was a legendary figure in the boxing game. He fought the greatest of his time, early in the century. He was esteemed as the most cagey of all the fighters— foxy to a shocking degree. Kid McCoy admitted he was smart. He gloated in the dodges and shifty stratagems he employed.

His favorite story told how, during a boxing tour in South Africa, he knocked out the King of the Kaffirs. This was a giant aboriginal black, a tribesman of prodigious size and strength, who was being groomed as a prizefighter. Kid McCoy himself was nothing more than a middleweight, a mere pigmy beside the King of the Kaffirs. He saw the ebony giant do some boxing in training, and noticed that he was barefoot. The King of the Kaffirs could not accommodate himself to shoes. In all his bouts he boxed the barefoot way.

So Kid McCoy got himself some carpet tacks, gave a handful to one of his seconds and told him to toss them into the ring, at a signal from the Kid. When the

73

bell rang, out came the King of the Kaffirs, a monster, a Goliath. The pigmy Kid danced about him for a moment, gave the signal, and the seconds tossed the handful of tacks into the middle of the ring. The King of the Kaffirs made a rush at his puny adversary, but stopped suddenly with an expression of pain. Ouch! And he reached down to take a tack out of his kingly foot. At that moment Kid McCoy knocked him out.

Such was the cunning of the Kid, who from boxing proceeded to still more gaudy adventures. He dissipated a large fortune. The quarter of a million he had earned in the ring went through his fingers in madcap fashion. He was married nine times. He remarried the same woman four times. Sentimental follies culminated in crime, when the Kid killed a sweetheart of his. A wild quarrel of love and jealousy, and then the deed of blood. He was sent to prison for the crime of passion, and emerged after years—middle-aged, a shadow of the Kid so wise in the prize ring and so foolish on the rose-covered field of romance.

Dying a suicide, he left a message to young men, advising them to live cleanly, behave themselves. The Kid, who was so wise and cagey, found this wild world too much for him. He wrote this last explanation: "Sorry, I could not endure this world's madness!" Too mad even for the wise, mad, smart, foolish Kid McCoy!

In a Paris court a judge spoke words of wisdom—not such original wisdom, but mighty close to the point. "Never," he declared, "never arouse a woman's jealousy. It is a very dangerous thing to do!"

The magistrate was passing sentence on a young bookkeeper who had tried that folly—arousing a woman's jealousy. Fernand Prevost was in love with Yvonne Hombert. He thought she liked his friend, Georges Lavaud, too much. So one day he said to her, "Oh, tonight I have an important rendezvous. I am taking a girl to the cinema—a beautiful girl." Thereby he sought to arouse the jealousy of Yvonne.

He had no date with any girl. Instead of taking a beautiful mademoiselle to the cinema, he went to the apartment of his friend, Georges, to talk things over. When he entered he observed that his friend was embarrassed. He happened to notice a curtain. Beneath the curtain he saw two little feet in charming slippers. He rushed to the curtain, tore it aside—and there was Yvonne.

He had made her jealous and she had taken her revenge. She had cherished no particular concern for friend Georges, and had given herself to him only for revenge, Parisian style. In fatal style—because in a moment the maddened young bookkeeper stood with a smoking revolver in his hand. Later he was tried for the murder of his friend and Yvonne.

So it was that the magistrate sagely remarked: "Never arouse a woman's jealousy. It is a very dangerous thing to do." Then he sentenced the young bookkeeper to five years of solitary confinement.

In France there was quite a bit of talk about the fact that there was no law to regulate the sale of firearms. Anybody could buy any sort of weapon he might want without any questions being asked. Some people complained that it was altogether too common for ladies to walk into a store and buy a gun with which to shoot an unfaithful husband or sweetheart. And the folks who believed there ought to be a law pointed to the story of Alice Francois.

Alice's husband left her. Wild with the rage of a woman scorned, she went to a gunsmith and bought a pistol. She told the gunsmith to be sure that the pistol was loaded. Then she looked up her husband and found him talking to a beautiful blonde. Alice drew the pistol from her handbag and opened fire on hubby and the blonde. She fired six times. It sounded like a pitched battle, but nothing happened. The husband didn't fall—neither did the blonde.

The explanation pointed to the fact that, since there was no law about selling pistols, some of the French gunsmiths used psychology. The man who sold Alice the pistol noticed that she was agitated and figured she was going to shoot somebody. So he carefully loaded her gun with blanks. The police arrested Alice, but inasmuch as she hadn't shot anybody they gave her a bawling out and let her go.

She went straight to another gunsmith and bought another pistol. This time she made sure it wasn't loaded with any blanks. She made perfectly certain it had bullets in it, deadly bullets. Then she looked up her husband, and found him with that blonde again.

Once more she aimed the pistol at them. Once more she pulled the trigger six times, and once more nothing happened. There wasn't even any noise.

The second gunsmith had also used psychology. He, too, figured that Alice was going to shoot somebody, and when she insisted on having real bullets in the gun he secretly put the pistol out of commission. He filed off the firing pin. I'd like to have seen Alice's face as she kept pulling away at the trigger—all in vain.

This time the gendarmes thought that Alice had achieved enough attempted homicide, so they sent her to jail to cool off and calm down.

In Vienna, Herr Hedwig suffered from insomnia. At night he tossed and turned from one side to the other; he got out of bed and took a walk.

"Why don't you try hypnotism?" his wife suggested again and again.

Herr Hedwig didn't believe in hypnotism, but finally decided to try anything to get a couple of winks of sleep.

"All right," he conceded to his wife. "Get a hypnotist." And the wife did.

She brought in a man with the piercing eyes and fixed gaze of a mesmerist. He was a hypnotist all right. His hypnotism sure did work. He made passes in front of Herr Hedwig's face and droned hypnotic phrases of suggestion: "You are very sleepy. You are very sleepy. You are very sleepy."

And then as Herr Hedwig began to drowse away, the hypnotist tossed in an extra suggestion. "When you wake up don't ask your wife where she has been. Don't ask her. Don't ask her. Don't ask her."

Herr Hedwig declared later that the hypnotism was so powerful he found it impossible to disobey the suggestions, impossible to stay awake, impossible to ask his wife where she had been. Even when friends told him they had seen her out with the hypnotist night after night, at dance halls and cabarets, he still couldn't ask any questions. He was burning with jealousy, but was unable to question the wife.

The hypnotist, however, had forgotten one thing. He should have added as he made those mesmerizing passes: "Don't sue for a divorce; don't sue for a divorce; don't sue for a divorce."

But, as he didn't do that, Herr Hedwig sued for a divorce in the Vienna courts.

The front page carried a surprise headline concerning the co-author of "The Front Page," that dashing play of newspaper life which was a smash hit some years ago. The surprise headline was: "Suit dismissed at the request of plaintiff." Miss Carol Frink, Chicago dramatic critic and first wife of Charles MacArthur, called off her hundred-thousand-dollar suit for alienation of affections against Helen Hayes, star actress and second wife of Charles MacArthur. The trial had begun, and all sorts of vivacious proceedings had ensued, when in the middle of the high jinks Carol Frink informed the judge that she didn't desire the hundred thousand. All she wanted was satisfaction—not money. She had had her satisfaction, and that ended it.

A sprightly lot of satisfaction it had been. Highly diverting testimony, sentimental letters read into the record and gales of laughter sweeping the courtroom —which was jammed with an élite crowd eager to see and hear the famous personalities in a parade of romantic difficulties. Beguiling pictures were drawn of a famous playwright gone acourting—his blithesome way of wooing, wooing his first wife, also his second. Romance of a newspaper office, with tender phrases exchanged at the water cooler.

Impoverished young newspaperman and newspaper woman get married, but the marriage doesn't last. The newspaperman rises to stage fame and fortune. Romance Number Two, with the famous actress. It began at a party. He was eating peanuts and he offered her some, saying he wished they were emeralds. "Goober gems," one tabloid called those peanuts.

In the courtroom Charlie MacArthur took it with a grin when they read aloud his love letters of long ago. And rollicking love letters they were. In one he spoke of his "violin case feet"—tramping up Broadway in feverish pursuit of "hundreds of affrighted virgins." He wasn't embarrassed when they read that. It was a sort of sentimental phraseology to be expected of a cynical wit. But the author of the hard-boiled newspaper drama did wince when it was disclosed

79

that he had signed one of his lovelorn epistles with the following: "One thousand times one million X-X-X." The X's of course meant kisses. He admitted he had sent all those kisses, and commented with an uncomfortable squirming, "It sounds to me like 1930." Dear departed younger days of 1930.

That was the sort of satisfaction the plaintiff had for three days in court. So then she asked the judge to call off the hilarious proceedings and dismiss her hundred-thousand-dollar suit, and His Honor did—agreeing that it was an ample amount of satisfaction.

Any reporter would smell a story on seeing the following—a newspaper advertisement, one of the melancholy kind in which a husband advertises he will not be responsible for his wife's debts. It read in the familiar traditional form, with a kicker. "My wife," it announced, "having left my bed and board—and absconded with my flute." Yes, she ran away with the family piccolo.

John Oresky told a sad story. He was a musician, his instrument the flute. He had played with Sousa, he had tooted on the flute with the greatest bands and orchestras. But married life was not such perfect harmony. His wife ran away from him, taking the flute, eloping with the piccolo. The musician showed the reporters closets full of women's clothes. No, she didn't take her clothes with her when she left. She didn't take anything, except the flute. She clasped the piccolo to her and fled.

"It's because she is jealous," moaned the musician, "jealous of that flute. She hates the piccolo."

It was a magnificent four-hundred-dollar instrument that played the most beautiful melodies. The musician was devoted to it, blowing his soul into the mouthpiece and fingering his heart away on the silver keys.

"She is jealous of my art, my music," he sighed.

His art and music were symbolized by the flute, a human life expressed by a piccolo. We were never informed what the jealousy-crazed woman did with her hated rival, the four-hundred-dollar musical instrument.

In Detroit a man appealed to the police, asking them to find his wife. He related how wifie had left him, vanished. Why did wifie abandon her hubby? That was made clear by a promise he asked the cops to relay.

"Tell her I won't do it again," he said fervently, and explained: "I'll admit I was making eyes at the lady next door. But I promise I won't do it again. I won't even glance at that lady next door."

A pathetic story, and to make it completely heartbreaking we must add this one detail: hubby and wifie were of the same age—seventy-one.

Love is an old, old story—not that the lady fair in this love story from Findlay, Ohio, was old. She was thirty-one, which you'd hardly call aged or senescent. The two rivals for her affections, however, were sixty-three and eighty, respectively—which makes it an old, old story indeed. You might think the younger man to have been the preferred suitor—the mere youth of sixty-three. Not at all. It was the old boy of eighty who was lucky in love.

The fight began when the sixty-three-year-old suitor charged the lady of thirty-one with showing less affection toward himself than toward the suitor of eighty. They argued from words to blows. The sexagenarian grabbed a bread knife and took a swipe at the octogenarian, inflicting a cut in his back. Whereupon the lady of thirty-one picked up the butter dish, and broke it over the sexagenarian's head, inflicting a deep scalp wound.

This old, old story ended with two of the participants in jail and one in the hospital.

At Harvard two undergraduates fought a duel with mighty swords, the Homeric weapons of Grecian warriors. Harvard was staging a classic play in which the heroine was Cassandra, the legendary lady of Grecian myth. The Harvard Cassandra was Miss Marie Herrara. In the play, one of the Greek warriors took Cassandra in his arms—and slew her.

Two students alternated in the hugging, homicidal rôle. In one performance the embrace of death was assigned to Milos Safranek, son of a Jugoslav official at Washington. In the next performance Jefferson Duffield was chosen. The two got into a row about it, and fought for the privilege of holding the damsel in their arms and slaying her—stage play. We were not told which was the most fascinating—the holding or the slaying.

In the impromptu duel both students were costumed as Greek warriors—helmets, shields, swords and all. They battled it out the way the heroes of Homer used to do—with the clashing of sword on helmet and shield. Luckily, the weapons were theatrical prop swords, made of wood—but they were ponderous. The two duelists couldn't behead each other—it was more like socking with heavy clubs, more Neanderthal than Homeric.

Other students tried to separate them—and were almost beaned by the swinging swords. So furious were the classic duelists that the peacemakers could only get them apart by dousing them with buckets of water. That ended it, with the question still undecided—who would take Cassandra in his arms and slay her?

The following lively story takes us into the lofty atmosphere of society, among the bluebloods and the élite. The gentleman who was the hero was wealthy, in the Social Register, a member of exclusive clubs, and moreover he was a colonel. The colonel lived as you'd expect, on Park Avenue—in the fifties, in the most aloof part of that aristocratic boulevard. That's Park Avenue as is Park Avenue.

In his magnificent apartment the colonel was entertaining—and in a big way. He was host to seven young ladies. That was socially correct, because the number seven occurred in the colonel's age. He was sixty-seven. The beverages were of the best. The champagne was of the vintage of 1926, one of the rarest vintage years La Belle France had ever known.

A good time was being had by all until, sad to relate, two of the girls got into a fight—cause, jealousy—two beauties rivals in love. And with this, the Park Avenue salon was in an uproar. The two ladies, one a brunette and the other a redhead, were in each other's hair—dark brown and titian, respectively. The colonel tried to separate them. As he did so, the girls started swinging bottles. The brunette crowned the redhead with a champagne bottle, vintage of 1926. The bottle shattered—it was lucky it was empty. It cut a big gash in the titian-tinted scalp. Whereupon the redhead swung with a ginger-ale bottle. She crowned the brunette—also the colonel. She bounced the bottle off the graceful brow of one and the venerable dome of the other. Graceful brow and venerable dome sustained deplorable injuries.

The fracas ended in the police court, with the colonel and the two beautiful battlers under arrest. The cops looked into their records. The colonel's record was all gilt-edge Social Register. As for the redhead, the annals of the police had her charted this way: Arrested 1928, disorderly conduct, six months in the workhouse. November, 1928, vagrancy, six weeks. June, 1936, intoxication and disorderly conduct, et cetera, et cetera.

Such was the story of the colonel's party, in which the sixty-seven-year-old socialite undertook to entertain seven young ladies—he certainly knew how to pick 'em.

IV

Medley of Misadventure

It is notable how many different kinds of trouble can flourish in the rosy realm of romance—odd disturbances; peculiar modes of discord, singular twists of rumpus and row. Somewhere in ancient Greek comedy there is a sad wight· who gives theological proof, saying: "I know the gods exist—they treat me so badly." So it is perhaps a tribute to Aphrodite's divinity that she can devise misadventures so surprising, and treat her devotees badly in such strange ways.

❧

At Los Angeles, they solved what they called the Red Rose Murder. The police arrested a hunted fugitive. He confessed. They quoted him as saying, "I'm glad I'm caught. I've been going through torture."

Alice Burns was a young woman who frequented a cocktail bar. She was what they called a percentage girl. She drank with men, persuaded them to buy—and got a percentage of the bar checks they paid. One night she sat drinking with a man, laughing and chatting, and persuading him to order more and more highballs. He was getting quite drunk, but that was all a part of the business of a percentage girl in a cocktail bar. One thing especially she noted—he had a great big roll of bills. So she accepted an invitation to take a drive with him in his car. He was much the worse off for liquor, but a percentage girl didn't mind that. So away they drove.

The man, when he confessed, was quoted as saying, "We were both having a good time until we got into an argument over something—I don't remember what." It was the drunkenness that the percentage girl had encouraged. In his alcoholic rage he stabbed and killed her.

She was found on the highway, and beneath her was a red rose—it had been torn from her coat in the struggle. So they called it the Red Rose Murder. The killer fled, driving as fast as he could, haunted by conscience, haunted by fear. So when it was all over he said, "I'm glad I'm caught. I've been going through torture."

87

PAGEANT OF ROMANCE

A somber, repellent story, telling powerfully of folly, evil and retribution—and the red rose.

🐚

Here was the weirdest shocker the news had brought in a long time. In Canada, at Sudbury, Ontario, John Basok, a section hand, wanted to dance. He asked a waitress in the place of entertainment. She refused. Whereupon the section hand whipped out a gun and opened fire, shooting the waitress five times. She fell to the floor. The section hand, dashing to escape, stumbled over her, fell—and broke his neck. The girl, badly wounded, recovered.

🐚

When a caballero serenades his lady you know how it is, Señor. He is full of sentiment—he is full of fire. Do not interrupt a caballero when he strums his guitar and sings his love song.

At Chihuahua City in Mexico, Lieutenant Jose Martinez of the Chihuahua military garrison, was in love with a beautiful señorita. He saw her, he sighed, and he made passionate advances—the way you make them according to old Spanish custom. At night he took his guitar, placed himself beneath the window of his love and sang a serenade.

He was singing soulfully when the chief of police came along. The chief went politely to the lieutenant and said:—"But, Señor, your permit."

"Permit?" exclaimed the lovelorn lieutenant.

The chief of police explained: "But, yes." It seems there was a law, a most unromantic law, which required that a caballero must get out a permit before he is permitted to serenade his señorita under her window. A lovesick-serenading permit, something like a peddler's permit or a dog license.

The response of the enamored lieutenant was emphatic. He pulled out his pistol, and shot the chief of police. You understand, Señor—one should not interrupt a caballero as he serenades the lady of his heart.

The chief of police, critically wounded, went to the hospital. The romantic lieutenant fled to the hills, possibly intending to take up the career of a bandit— à la Pancho Villa. Our heart goes out to the caballero.

In the city of Milan, in Italy, a young man and woman were arrested because of suspicions of robbery. And were they happy about it? Were they relieved? I'll leave it to you to judge their feelings.

The girl was a housemaid. Her employer noticed that a young man was frequently around. That raised his suspicion of collusion between the two for purposes of robbery. When they were arrested they explained to the police—they were engaged to be married. The young man was unemployed, and the girl was trying to get him odd jobs until times got better and they could marry.

The police, in checking their story, found that unknown to the two themselves, they were brother and sister. As children of refugees during the Austrian invasion of Italy in the first World War, they had become separated and had drifted apart until they happened to meet in Milan, neither knowing who the other was.

If you feel that you have a knack of getting into complications, consider the case of Frank Neubauer of Chicago. Frank got tangled in a matrimonial maze that was outlined graphically in a court decision handed down by a bewildered judge. His Honor decreed that Frank's first wife was not his wife, nor was his second wife, and neither was Frank's sister his wife, although she was sentenced to jail for marrying her brother. So Frank was declared a single man, although he had married two wives, had also married his sister, and had become the father of a daughter, then a year old.

How did they unravel those complications? It was like this: First Frank married his sister. Sounds mighty bad, and it was because Frank's fiancée was too busy at work to take time off to get married. She was a Rumanian, and somebody told her that it was an old American custom to have marriage performed by proxy—somebody else taking the place of the bride, a stand-in.

Frank's sister agreed to be the proxy. She filled in as the bride at the wedding and neglected to tell the judge who performed the wedding that she was only a stand-in. The ceremony was performed as the real thing, and the sister was legally her brother's wife— or she would have been except for the fact that she was already married. For this mix-up and deception, the sister, when the judge untangled the complexities, was sentenced to twenty-four hours in jail.

The marriage by proxy not counting, Frank was legally a single man. According to law, it was all right when he went ahead and got married again. He was single, but unfortunately his bride was not. She was married, having neglected to get a divorce from her husband.

By this time I think you will echo the sentiments of the Chicago judge who tried the case. When the facts were presented to him, he said: "Wait a minute, till I catch my breath." When he did, he pronounced all the marrying illegal and said Frank would have to marry his latest wife all over again—which Frank said he would do. And in a hurry—because he was about to be taken into the Army.

❦

At St. Louis the authorities appealed to the Navy Department in a case complex with legal angles—also human angles. A sixteen-year-old girl was charged with bigamy. Her first husband had been a sailor aboard an American warship in the Battle of the Java Sea.

Mary Haislip was fifteen years old when she worked in the home of Mrs. Williams as a maid. Mrs. Williams' son, Robert, joined the Navy. But first, he married Mary, his mother's maid. He went to training camp—then off to the Far East. There Robert Williams vanished in the swirling events of war. The Navy Department sent word to his mother and wife that he was listed as missing in the Battle of the Sea of Java.

Mary, now sixteen, was sure he was dead. She met another young man, a twenty-one-year-old operator of a doughnut shop. He was sympathetic to her story—and they fell in love and were married. Whereupon the mother-in-law, Mrs. Williams, had Mary arrested for bigamy.

In court, the girl wailed: "I just know he is dead."

The mother spoke with firm conviction: "I just know he is alive."

The authorities could only appeal to the Navy Department for some further ruling concerning the fate of Sailor Robert Williams, who vanished in the Battle of the Sea of Java.

Sailor Edwin Schumacker of the Merchant Marine was torpedoed twice. Once off Nova Scotia the explosion that sank the ship knocked him into the sea—with the ship's compass still in his hands. Then he drifted for five days in a lifeboat. The Navy afterward gave him an official commendation—because of the way he kept up the courage of his fellow survivors by telling them stories and singing them songs.

No doubt they were songs about Betty, sixteen-year-old Betty Peynado in New York.

Then came a voyage that was uneventful at sea but was followed by difficulties on land. When Sailor Schumacker got safely ashore he started off to see Betty. That promised nothing but happiness, joy and delight, but it turned out to be an adventure rather worse than being torpedoed by Nazi U-boats. The sailor was paid off in Boston, got ninety-eight dollars. Betty was in New York, and Sailor Schumacker was a frugal sort of mariner. To save railroad fare he hitch-hiked a ride on a truck. Near the big town the truck driver robbed him, and tossed him out onto the highway.

The unlucky sailor, left penniless, started walking. He hiked down to the headquarters of the National Maritime Union, and there he found a letter from Betty. So he went to see her, but she and her family were not home. He left a note for her, killed some time, and returned. Still nobody home. He left another note, and again waited.

The hapless mariner was tired, worn out. Desperately needing some sleep, he decided to get into the apartment of Betty and her family and take a nap. He figured he could enter by the fire escape and through a window. That was where Sailor Schumacker made his biggest mistake.

He picked the wrong window, and climbed into the apartment of Mrs. Carrie Kleinman, who was indeed surprised to see the hero of two torpedoings at sea. She screamed and called the police, and the unhappy sailor was taken off to jail as a burglar.

93

The next day his story was told in court, and to prove his innocence Betty appeared—with the two notes that he had left for her. One of these told her that he would haunt her home until she appeared. Getting in and going to sleep seemed pretty much like haunting, and the judge dismissed the case.

All of which proves that for a sailor, life on land can be worse than the U-boat-infested ocean. Take me back to those torpedoes!

Now here's a question: "If George Washington's socks fall down, how could a fifty-year-old man hold the love of a young woman of twenty-four?"

That conundrum was suggested by the proceedings in the McKee divorce trial at Los Angeles. The wife in the case alleged that her husband confessed to her his deep affection for a young lady called "Muffy." Telling his wife about it, he gave her a glowing description of Muffy. In the words of testimony in court, he said that she was "a great beauty, and wealthy, and had diamonds and castles in England." Who wouldn't fall in love with Muffy—with her beauty, her diamonds and her castles?

He took Muffy to the Mardi Gras at New Orleans, and that's where we come to the question of George Washington and the socks. The wife testified: "My husband said he had gone to the ball dressed as George

Washington but that he was embarrassed because his socks had fallen down."

The court testimony came to a soulful culmination when hubby told wifie he was worried about retaining the affections of Muffy—with her beauty, her diamonds and her castles. He asked wifie for advice about it—"how to hold on to a girl of twenty-four like Muffy," as wifie expressed it. And wifie obligingly told him. She didn't say just what, but maybe it was: "George Washington, keep your socks up."

There was a new turn in the peculiar history of the American heiress, Merry Fahrney, who was reported to be an admirer of Nazi Germany and who was in the Argentine. She got herself to South America by purchasing a marriage ceremony as a way to get a passport. Not able to procure one of the American variety, she paid a waiter, a Swedish citizen, fifteen hundred dollars to marry her, and that enabled her to take out a Swedish passport. Soon afterward she divorced the waiter, and left the country.

This was followed by stories that the heiress so anxious to get out of the United States was a pro-Nazi, and thereupon things followed thick and fast for her. The money she inherited was a patent medicine fortune left her by her grandfather, and moves were made to tie up the cash. The waiter who went through the marriage ceremony with her, sued to make her pay him a hundred thousand dollars. Moreover, there were court proceedings to annul the divorce she got from him, and these brought about the new twister in the case.

The patent medicine heiress was known to have been friendly with a Nazi diplomatic official in Washington before America's entrance into the war, and in court the judge said: "The divorce apparently was planned and conceived by some very clever people." He added that, in view of her reported relationships with German diplomats, "it seems quite possible they arranged the marriage, utilizing their knowledge of citizenship laws." So the strange case of the lady who inherited the patent medicine money had Nazi diplomatic angles.

She, meanwhile, was in Buenos Aires—much perturbed and issuing statements.

One of the strangest of amnesia stories was told in Hollywood—the case of a woman who found herself married to a man she didn't know.

At night Mrs. Gloria Weller Miller, twenty-five years old, was driving along in her car. Some sudden realization came to her, and she saw that she was driving a blue sedan. That surprised her—because the car that she and her husband owned was gray. She said to herself, "I wonder where I got this blue car?"

Then she noticed that the scene about her was unfamiliar. A city, but it was not the place where her

96

home was—not Atascadero, California. Still more puzzled, she stopped and asked, and was told that she was in Hollywood. That was two hundred miles from Atascadero.

Realizing that something strange indeed had occurred, she wired her home town and asked for information about her husband and herself, Mr. and Mrs. Pierce Weller. She was informed that Pierce Weller, a fifty-year-old retired newspaper editor, had died in November of the previous year. Sudden death —his wife finding the body. Then in May, Mrs. Weller had remarried, and become Mrs. Henry Miller of Hollywood.

The baffled woman knew nothing about these things —she Mrs. Henry Miller? She was Mrs. Pierce Weller. Her husband dead? She married again? Utterly bewildered, she went to the police, and asked them to clear up the mystery. They took her to Henry Miller. She did not recognize him. "I never saw him before in my life," she said.

Henry Miller told her that he had met her at the horse races in Agua Caliente, Mexico, and they had been married at Las Vegas, Nevada. They had lived together ever since, and she had left their home that evening in their car. She recalled nothing of this. The last thing she remembered was her home with her first husband. It was a case of amnesia produced by shock. Her memory had gone blank with the shock of finding her first husband dead.

To newspapermen reporting the singular drama she exclaimed: "Look at me. I have bleached blond hair, but before I had pretty red hair. I don't like myself as a blonde."

She said that her second husband, the man she did not know, was very sympathetic about it all. He offered to give her a divorce if she so desired.

And we can only wonder—what did she do? Did she so desire? The news never told.

⁂

The following strange case of a professor at the University of Wisconsin is one that would have beguiled the dreams of the fantastic French writer, Marcel Proust. It is a tale of a phobic prison, and to it Proust might have devoted volumes of his prolix and introverted prose. That mad French novelist was himself a victim of a strange phobia. For years he shunned the light, an enemy of the sun. He left his room only at night, when it was dark. He passed his days in hermit seclusion, in a room with heavy shades drawn. Even an electric light terrified him. His life was illuminated only by the dim glow of candles. And his room was sound-proof—for greater seclusion.

At the University of Wisconsin, Professor William Mallory Leonard, a poet of talent, was haunted by the terror of distances—agoraphobia. He never left the campus of the university. To journey four or five blocks from his house brought a spasm of horror upon him. He lived and taught and wrote in what he called a phobic prison. A familiar figure, distinguished by glowing, gaudy Oxford ties; and sometimes he wore a blazing red bathing suit. Odd professor, odd poet.

I suppose you'd call his love story a phobic romance. A young woman student became attracted to his strangely imaginative poetry. She became acquainted with him. He was thirty years older than she, but she fell in love with him—and she thought she could cure him of his psychic malady, his horror of distances. They were married, and it seemed that love indeed had triumphed over phobia.

The young bride took the old professor by the hand and led him away from the campus, led him on and on, block after block, out into open country, the woods and the fields. And he felt no fright, no horror of all the distance. He was overjoyed. He thought he was cured of the haunting terror that had afflicted him since childhood.

But as time and marriage went on, the phobia returned. No longer could his wife take him by the hand, lead him away from the campus, devoid of fear. His old terror was back upon him, just as before. When phobia came back through the door, love flew out of the window.

Presently the wife left the professor. She accused him of trying to make her feel insane—an odd thing to do to your wife. Wives usually seem flighty enough as it is. She got a divorce, but canceled it, and returned to the professor, returned to his phobic prison. It didn't work out, it was the same as before. Maybe the professor once again tried to make his wife feel insane. There was another separation. The news of the case ended with a picture of the wife of the phobic prisoner

99

trying to make up her mind whether to leave him for good or return once more.

🐚

In Colorado a girl was released from jail, and emerged with the explanation: "Fine—just as I expected. I am cured—no wedding bells for me!" She had had herself sent to jail to keep from getting married.

At the holiday season Margaret Caro, seventeen years old, appeared in a juvenile court and asked the judge to put her behind bars until after January 20. That, she explained, was the day set for her wedding. She related that she was engaged to be married to a man much older than herself. She didn't want to marry him, but she just couldn't help it, just couldn't resist him when she was in his presence. He had some sort of fatal charm. So she asked the judge to put her in a cell and keep her there, so she could be away from him and thus break the spell.

That's the way it all turned out. The judge sent Margaret to jail and she was released—cured. At least, she said so—though you couldn't tell what might happen when she met that aged, cooing wooer again.

🐚

Here's the story of a man who tried to create a perfect wife. The information comes, as you might expect, from a divorce court. The would-be creator of the ideal mate was a psychologist and psychoanalyst. He was fifty-two, thirty years older than the wife whom he sought to endow with all perfections for matrimony.

In a Los Angeles court it was told how the psychologist, Doctor Negri, molded the young woman's mind and guided her thoughts, to make her the perfect wife. Then he married her—and once the wedding ring got on the finger the psychoanalysis didn't seem to work so well. The scientific doctor stated that the perfect wife refused to wash the dishes. She would not sweep the house. Often the doctor had to take care of the baby.

The wife charged that the psychoanalyzing doctor was not so perfect as a husband. She declared that although he made ten thousand dollars a year, he gave her only twenty-five cents a day for spending money.

That was what happened to the marriage of the psychoanalyzing psychologist and the perfect wife that he created. The doctor explained the reason. He said that when he started out on the miracle he made just one mistake—he forgot to psychoanalyze himself. I suppose he meant that anybody who thinks he can create a perfect wife is just plain crazy.

🙢

George Schermann of Jamaica, Long Island, had an enthusiasm for the loftier branches of knowledge. But George, with all his erudition, got married to a seventeen-year-old bride. He was exceedingly good to her—in his learned fashion. He told her to devote her spare time to what was described in these words: "a study of the philosophies and teachings of Plato, Aristotle and Socrates." He made her stop reading magazines and current literature. As for the funnies—absolutely no! Not one glimpse at "Little Orphan Annie" or "Bringing Up Father" or "Joe Palooka." Nothing but Plato, Aristotle and Socrates.

Hubby grew indignant when seventeen-year-old wifie found these philosophers, as she herself explained, "uninteresting and difficult." He said she'd have to peruse the Symposium of Plato, whether she liked it or not, the logical works of Aristotle, whether she understood them or not, and the dialectics of Socrates, although they might tie her brains in a knot. All of which was hardly in accordance with the maxim, "be kind to dumb brides."

Wifie sued for a divorce, seeking to break the bonds of matrimony with her husband, and Plato and Aristotle and Socrates.

A classic of radio is the story of a New Jersey policeman who took a lady for a ride in his police radio car—and all the time he had his transmitter on. So, unknown to themselves, the policeman and the lady were on the air as they had a chat. They were giving a broadcast. People who happened to be listening in on that wave length were much astonished by the unrehearsed program.

The calamitous cop came up for trial at Milburn, New Jersey. There were six charges against him, one of which was "conduct unbecoming an officer and a gentleman." The courtroom was packed, because it was hoped that the testimony would repeat what the policeman and the lady said to each other while on the air. A lot of people who missed the memorable broadcast wanted to hear it reproduced in court. They were disappointed. There was no testimony at all, for the pathetic policeman made no defense. He pleaded guilty.

He confessed that while out in his radio car he had communicated with police headquarters, and forgot to switch off the transmitter. Then a young lady asked him to take her to the railroad station to catch a train. He said they were driving along and chatting about this and that. You know, he said this and she said that. The conversation was well worth hearing, as was affirmed by those who were lucky enough to be listening in. The cop's confession concluded with these melancholy words: "On the way I was stopped by another radio car and advised that my transmitter was on." That was the painful moment.

What was the penalty imposed on the hapless cop? It happened that three times in the past he had won decorations for bravery—before he mustered courage to give a lady a ride. The court took cognizance of his record for heroism, and let him off with a five-hundred-dollar fine and the loss of his days off for the next four months. He kept his job as a policeman—resolving that thereafter he'd keep a wary eye on the radio transmitter, and if a young lady asked him for a ride he'd say no.

🌾

At Boston the authorities suspended a lady's automobile driving license because of a kiss. She was speeding along in her car at night without lights. Of course, it is known that shrinking damsels often do like to have the lights out, but this should not apply to an automobile on the highway. She was buzzing along at forty-five miles an hour, but the kiss she bestowed on the man next to her wasn't nearly as fast as that. It lasted for five minutes, testified the police. It lasted while the car went whizzing along for nearly four miles—and without lights.

The case came up before the appropriate Solomon, Boston's Motor Vehicle Commissioner Frank A. Godwin, and he handed down this magisterial decree: "Osculation," he ruled, "should be performed only when the car is stopped." But suppose you're in a hurry, Commissioner? Suppose a fellow is rushing home to the wife? If he stopped the car for five minutes he might be late, and that might make the wife angry.

The Commissioner suspended the lady's license for one week, and uttered an opinion worthy of Solomon. "She should be able to get the kissing out of her system in the next seven days," quoth the Commissioner. She could perform her osculation five minutes at a time as often as she liked for seven days—but not while driving the car, lady, not while driving the car.

🌾

Have you ever, when out driving, been stopped by a traffic cop who tried to sell you some tickets to a policemen's benefit? No doubt you have, and very likely you have purchased a couple. I have. Perhaps you hadn't the slightest desire to attend the policemen's benefit, but you know how it is. Dr. Michael J. O'Brien of New York knew how it was, and he waxed indignant about it.

Dr. O'Brien, seventy years old and described not as a physician but as a historian, was driving along down in Florida at Hialeah, and violated a traffic rule. The cop told him the traffic violation would be squared if the doctor would purchase two one-dollar tickets for the Hialeah Firemen's and Policemen's Benefit.

"I told him," the doctor afterward related, "that I would buy one ticket, but that I couldn't use two."

The cop responded: "Yes, you can. It's easy to pick up a babe."

That was what irked the doctor—"easy to pick up a babe." He made this following plaintive comment, "And mind you, I am seventy years old."

All of which put a new light on the moonlit subject of love and romance—the idea of picking up a babe for the purpose of being able to use two tickets for the Firemen's and Policemen's Benefit.

🦋

A nudist stowaway was deported from Texas. Mrs. Esther Worman was sent back to England —fully clothed. The sartorial part of it was all right by

Mrs. Esther Worman, because she became a nudist in spite of herself.

She stowed away on a ship to come to America. A plump and prepossessing blonde, her motive was to look for her husband. He was an English pugilist in the U.S.A., fighting in the ring some place in this broad land. The lady hid herself in the hold of the freighter. When out at sea it got mighty hot down there. It was near the engine room. It became so broiling hot that she was simply compelled to disrobe.

So there she was like Eve, when suddenly a fire broke out in the hold. She had to escape from the flames in a hurry—no time to dress. So she dashed up on deck, blond and plump, to the surprise of the sailors. I suppose she felt like jumping overboard, and the sailors like jumping overboard after her.

When the freighter put in at Galveston, the nudist stowaway was turned over to the immigration authorities. They condemned her to be deported—fully garbed, from shoes to hat.

There's a particularly low kind of criminal called a pants robber. He's the kind of crook who compels a victim to take off his trousers, the idea being that the victim in such condition of disapparel will not be able to dash down the street and give the alarm. It's a humiliating thing for a citizen to be forced to disrobe in such fashion, but when a bandit is pointing a gun at you what can you do?

Harold Olsen of Boston would undoubtedly have done nothing, would have obeyed. Harold, who was thirty-eight years old, would probably have yielded to the command of the pants robber, if it hadn't been for one thing. With Harold was the girl friend—and would he remove his trousers in her presence? Never—bandit or no bandit. It would have been entirely too embarrassing to Harold—also to the girl friend.

So, instead, he made a lunge at the robber, tackled him. In the ensuing fight, the criminal escaped. Harold sustained some bruises and cuts on his face, but his trousers remained firmly in place, much to his relief and that of the girl friend.

The most you could ask of a beauty contest winner would seem to be—is she beautiful? But that was an unsophisticated American point of view. Over in Europe a beauty contest included more than a dimpled chin, a swanlike neck and some tantalizing curves. Not that they demanded intellectual qualifications, erudition or brains in a beauty contest. That would be cruel and unusual. Nor did they consider such trivialities as morals. That would not be European. It was a case of politics. A girl had to have not only the right kind of knees and solar plexus and eyebrows, but also the right kind of politics.

This truth was brought to light with a flare of diplomatic proceedings at a beauty contest in London. Eighteen nations were represented by their queens of pulchritude, dazzling beauties all the way from the land of the reindeer to the realm of the camel of the desert. They were picking Miss Europa.

The trouble came when they invited the ambassadors from the various nations to attend and get an eyeful. First, the Russian ambassador refused. He admitted that Miss Russia had beautiful eyes and a form divine that really was divine. The trouble was with her politics. He was a Communist. She was an anti-Communist. He was a Red. She was a White—except for some small matter of lipstick and rouge.

Then the German ambassador said he wouldn't attend. That seemed odd when you considered that the German entrant in the world beauty contest was not only exceedingly lovely, but also a descendant of Immanuel Kant, Germany's greatest philosopher. What would Kant think of his descendant in the beauty contest? But the German ambassador wasn't bothered about that philosophic question. The fräulein was partly of Jewish blood, she was not one hundred per cent Aryan, and she was an anti-Nazi.

It seemed odd to drag politics into a beauty contest. You wouldn't drag beauty into a politics contest—not if the beauty could help it.

At Santa Monica, California, an explanation was given of a knife wound incurred by Commander Earl Winfield Spencer, U.S.N., retired. He was the first husband of the twice-divorced Duchess of Windsor.

At night the retired naval officer was taken to a hospital for treatment of a cut in his chest. The whole thing was kept secret, and looked mysterious—but then came an explanation. His present wife stated that it was an accident, all because of a bottle of ketchup that was hard to open.

"He was holding a ketchup bottle, trying to open it with a knife," Mrs. Spencer told the police. "The knife slipped," she added, "and stuck him in the chest." She said she got some bandages and antiseptic, saw the wound was bleeding badly, and called a doctor—whereupon the Duchess of Windsor's first husband was taken to the hospital.

V

The Romance of the Century

This mechanistic era, so prosy by its own confession, has been embellished by a romance that takes its place
among the most celebrated in history. Helen's face may have
burned the topless towers of Ilium, and the Serpent of the
Nile may have beguiled Rome in the person of a Caesar or
an Antony, and there have been personages of royalty and
state who have spurned power and rank for love of a woman,
but history gives no parallel to the renunciation of Edward
VIII. Never has such a sovereign of such a realm given up such
a crown to gain a wife.

The historic drama of Edward and Wallis Warfield has
surely a headlined place in any pageant of romance. Though,

of course, it is in every memory as of yesterday. I'll tell it as it came to us then, as it was disclosed by the news. I recited it from day to day on the radio, and have notes to consult. From these I have compiled the story.

Britain was stunned by the news of the royal romance. The story was famous everywhere else in the world, but in the King's own realm little or nothing had been published about Edward VIII and Mrs. Wallis Warfield Simpson. The British press had studiously and conspicuously avoided all reference to the friendship between the sovereign and the lady from Baltimore. Privately the editors had said: "We don't talk about His Majesty's private life." But that changed suddenly, and British newspapers finally had to break the story, and were singing a different tune. The King's private life was indeed public matter.

Edward VIII was one of the most popular monarchs who ever ascended a throne. Some vehemently supported him in his romance; others were coldly opposed —and they were the prevailing power. The hostility was not so much because Mrs. Simpson, though a British subject, was American-born, nor because she was a commoner. But she was a divorcée; and middle-class, church-going opinion in England was vehemently and rigidly set against the admission of divorced people into the royal family. Queen Victoria had laid down the rule that a divorced woman, even though an innocent party to the suit, could not even be received at court. This rule was quietly but firmly approved by English churchgoers.

The rumor gained currency that the King might abdicate. Prime Minister Stanley Baldwin, speaking for a unanimous Cabinet, advised him not to think of marrying Mrs. Simpson. If His Majesty insisted, the Cabinet threatened to resign.

Baldwin revealed to the House of Commons the conferences between himself and his sovereign. The picture presented was one of unswerving determination, a king who would not yield. Baldwin related how during the autumn he had received many inquiries from British subjects in the United States and American citizens of British origin, asking him about the stories appearing in American newspapers, reports about the King and Mrs. Wallis Warfield Simpson. The Prime Minister stated that he had been disquieted by the flood of rumor in the Trans-Atlantic press. So, of his own accord, he went to the King. This was in October.

He told Edward VIII how gossip about himself and Mrs. Simpson was spreading far and wide in America. He explained to the monarch that he was worried about the effect it would have in the British dominions—especially in Canada, which was getting its stories from the United States. Edward listened in friendly fashion. Baldwin asked him to consider the matter, not to make any reply just then, but to wait and think it over.

The next time the Prime Minister called on the King it was in November, at Buckingham Palace. Baldwin began the subject—spoke of the idea of the King's marriage to Mrs. Simpson. He said the nation would be against it. The King's wife would necessarily become queen, and the British Empire had a right to some say in the selection of its queen.

The King responded: "I am going to marry Mrs. Simpson, and I am prepared to go." From that determination he never swerved an inch, said Baldwin.

Subsequent meetings were pretty much of the same pattern—the Prime Minister begging the King not to abdicate but to renounce the marriage instead, and always meeting with that same changeless determination. The Prime Minister declared that there was never any ill-feeling, the King always friendly. In that same friendly way the royal determination proceeded by inevitable logic to the abdication.

The abdication address of Edward VIII was one of the greatest broadcasts of all time, a truly extraordinary thing in power, pathos and simplicity. The simplicity of great drama began with the opening five words of introduction, as the London announcer said: "His Royal Highness, Prince Edward." There was the theme —a king no longer. In the closing sign-off, the English announcer concluded with the words: "His ex-Majesty," ending on the same theme.

We who had heard him speak on the radio before, when he was Prince of Wales and when he was King, knew his voice—light and bright in those times. But those were happy times. Now we had a different tone of speech from His Royal Highness Prince Edward, His ex-Majesty. His voice was hoarse; it seemed about to break, as if choking for utterance. It sounded like the voice of a man in tears. It was supremely the voice of one who after heart searching and heart struggle, had given up the throne of the British Empire—for love, for a woman.

He said he had performed his last duty as King Emperor—meaning that he had signed his own abdication. He made it clear that his struggle had been within himself, not against his ministers, not strife between persons. He spoke with kindness toward Prime Minister Stanley Baldwin, said the ministers had always given him the fullest consideration, and declared that his decision was his own. He had made it within himself.

The drama of an empire rose to a soaring note of pathos when Edward embarked upon the theme that stood first in the eyes of the world. There was something confessional about it, as though he were making his confession to the British Empire. He said: "You must believe me when I tell you that I have found it impossible to carry this heavy burden and responsibility and to discharge my duties as a king as I would wish to do, without the help and support of the woman I love."

You can take all the great speeches on the stage, all the splendid declamations of the classical drama, and you'll find nothing to approach the poignant appeal of the man who spoke to the British Empire, one-fourth of the human beings on this earth, explaining how he had had to choose between the greatest crown on earth and the woman he loved, and of how he had determined to give up the crown and go into exile.

For exile it was. He revealed that when he said: "It may be some time before I return to my native land."

To his successor he declared his loyalty. This was at the beginning of the address. "I have been succeeded by my brother, the Duke of York. My first words must be to declare my allegiance to him. This I do with all my heart." He ended with these words: "And now we all have a new King. I wish him and you, his people, happiness and prosperity with all my heart. God bless you. God save the King."

So he stepped out of the empire, on his lips that phrase which was like an echo of Britain. Through the English centuries it rings, a lusty, cheering shout—"God save the King!" Never in British history was it uttered in so sad and broken a voice as it was spoken by His ex-Majesty.

What must have been his thoughts? He had been the world's darling as the glamorous Prince of Wales. He had become the most popular of kings. In the tense drama which he played out before the eyes of the world, what had been his impulses and motives? Millions of human beings tried to guess and surmise, as he abdicated. What to think about it all?

It wasn't hard for a sentimental species like the human race to understand what it was to be in love—but so deeply, so head-over-heels, so madly as to toss aside the most gorgeous of crowns? Most of us had never been infatuated like that. Or had we? Could it have been that the devotion of many an adoring bridegroom was such that, if it were thwarted by kingship, he'd fling away the crown? Could it have been that more than one of us in Edward's royal robes would have acted as he had done? That surely reduced the drama of the British Empire to the most sentimental simplicity.

In the contrary extreme, it might be argued that even without any romance, even without any Mrs. Wallis Warfield Simpson, Edward was likely to get into a constitutional crisis anyway. He was strong-willed, impatient of restraint, the sort that might inevitably rebel against dictation. He was always resentful of the formalities and the conventional rituals that hedged in royalty. He wanted personal freedom, and a king was not free—least of all a constitutional king. Even before he took the throne he told his ministers that his private life was his own. Could it be that his determination to marry Wally of Baltimore was something of a symbol of his desire to be free?

Perhaps analysts of the future may discover all these things: devoted love, chivalrous romance, impatience of restraint, desire for freedom.

VI

Coronation

In the royal romance of Edward VIII a culminating consequence was the coronation of George VI. It was the most glowing of all the events during that period that now seems so distant—before this world-wide war. As it happened, I covered that sacrament of British monarchy for the radio, and broadcast from London an account of the fabulous ceremonial. This was fresh from immediate memory. So perhaps I can do little better than repeat it from the program transcript.

※

This morning at dawn all London seemed to be in the streets. Between 6:00 and 8:00 A.M. more than a thousand automobiles unloaded lords and ladies of the realm and other dignitaries at the entrances to Westminster Abbey. Officers in scarlet and gold and tall bearskin busbies examined our invitations, and passed us on to other functionaries.

I thought I would be lucky just to have a seat in the Abbey, anywhere. London friends warned me that I would probably be behind a pillar, in some remote corner, where I could neither see nor hear. I had been told that all the best seats were reserved for peers and peeresses, visiting royalty, ambassadors, M. P.'s. Maybe someone accidentally gave me the wrong ticket. At any rate, I found myself sitting within a short distance of the high altar, the throne, the center of everything—in a gallery marked for "Guests of Royalty."

The doors of the Abbey were closed at eight, with the main ceremony, the arrival of the King and Queen, scheduled for eleven. This meant that we must sit there for three solid hours. It gave one a chance to get acquainted with one's neighbors. Yes, even at the most formal of all formal British functions. Tier upon tier of special seats had been erected from the floor to the roof of the Abbey, each seat exactly wide enough for one person. So you couldn't help getting acquainted with your neighbor.

I found myself between two peeresses. As the hours went by, discovering that I was a stranger, they introduced me all around. Right back of me sat one of the King's equerries, who had just returned from accompanying the Duke of Windsor, the man who was to have been crowned. He was with Edward on the trip to a chateau in France where the Duke joined the lady from Baltimore.

We were in the first gallery. Directly below us sat more than a thousand peers and peeresses in their red velvet and ermine robes and their diamond tiaras. Each held his coronet in his lap, ready to put it on one instant after the coronation. Directly opposite and only a short distance off was the large royal box. The first to take their seats there in the front row were the Earl and Lady Strathmore, parents of the new Queen, proudest parents in the world. Lady Strathmore was simply beaming.

Lady Gordon Moore and her husband, who is physician to the royal family, pointed out to me each important person entering, and told me about them: the Earl of MacDuff, the Marchioness of Milford Haven, the Duke of Northumberland, Lady Louise Mountbatten, the Duchess of Westminster, the Duchess of Marlborough, the Duchess of Beaufort, and so on. And there was I from Dutchess County, New York, feeling like Mark Twain's Yankee at the Court of King Arthur.

My noble neighbors told me about one peeress who didn't like the idea of being separated from her husband. The peeresses all sat directly below us in the north transept, the peers in a body just opposite in the south transept. Said Lady Plander: "Isn't it too bad that I cannot sit beside His Lordship!" "Why?" asked a friend. "Oh," answered Lady Plander, "His Lordship will so miss my little asides!"

Just a few seats to my left, all in scarlet robes, sat one of the most influential men in the empire, Sir John

Reith, head of the British Broadcasting Company. Sir John looked rather troubled for two reasons: first, because he is one of the tallest men in the empire and found great difficulty in accommodating his legs; second, because he was behind an immense pillar. Perhaps the Earl of Norfolk and his aides, who arranged the seating, thought the head of British radio should be content to hear and not see.

Among the arrivals in one of the early processions were the representatives of foreign countries. They included exotic personalities, such as Prince and Princess Chichibu of Japan and the Crown Prince of Saudi Arabia. I saw the face of a Central Asian official who had helped me on an expedition years ago, His Royal Highness, Sirdar Shah Wali Khan from Afghanistan. Down the center aisle of the Abbey came Dejazmatch Makonnen Idalkatcho, representative of the exiled Ethiopian emperor, Haile Selassie. His being invited was what caused Mussolini to decline to send any Italian royalty to the coronation. Incidentally, there is a rumor that the invitation to the dethroned Ethiopian Lion of Judah went out by accident. Just a slip.

As we sat looking over the Abbey the noble lady on one side of me gave a gasp and called my attention to one of her sex just across the transept. "Horrors!" said she. "Look, she has on an evening gown with a low back and without sleeves. What a faux pas!" Then she added: "Every lady here should have her arms and shoulders covered. Luckily she can't be seen by Queen Mary from the royal box! But she will be seen by many others. Most unfortunate! Oh dear, oh dear!"

Between 10:00 and 10:45 came the processions of the high Church dignitaries bringing the King and Queen's regalia, and a few minutes later the little princesses, Elizabeth and Margaret Rose, one on each side of the Princess Royal, sister of the King. Then the Duchesses of Gloucester and Kent; and a moment later the Connaughts and the Athlones; Princess Pat; the Queen of Norway; and then most stately of them all, Queen Mary, attended by the Duchess of Devonshire.

At the moment that the Dean of Westminster and the Bishops approached the high altar carrying the orb, the crowns and other regalia, the sun burst through the morning London fog and Lady Jefferies, sitting on one side of me, said: "Ah, queens' weather!" Then she whispered to me: "Poor Edward, it always rained when he did anything."

The lords and ladies in the Abbey were beginning to get hungry. I could see them rather furtively pulling sandwiches from beneath their ermine robes. Lady Jefferies, observing my interest in this, opened her handbag and from a gold box took some concentrated meat tablets, which she offered to me. You know, the sort of thing aviators and explorers sometimes carry in case of dire emergency. She said she learned this from the royal family. They always go prepared, she explained. I saw a certain powerful nobleman of radio-wireless fame pull a small bottle out of his velvet sleeve and rather sheepishly tilt and turn his face against the Abbey wall. Was it tea?

The doctor to the royal family, sitting with us, explained that certain facilities this time were far, far

more adequate than ever before at a British coronation. Consequently there was less fainting than at the
previous coronation of George V.

At eleven sharp we heard a roar from the street, indicating that the King and Queen had arrived. A few
moments later, General Sir George Jefferies, all in
gold and red, dropped into his seat beside us. He had
ridden down from Buckingham Palace just behind the
gold coach of state, he and two others: the Air Force
Chief Marshal on one side, Admiral the Earl of Cork
on the other, with General Sir George in the middle,
representing His Majesty's land forces. He said that the
King and Queen had been given an overwhelming re-
ception by the great crowds along the Mall, down
Whitehall, and near the Abbey.

All the while there was, of course, another member
of the House of Windsor not there in person, but in
everyone's thoughts. What if Edward were being
crowned? What would have happened had he and the
woman of his choice come riding in the golden coach?
A lady whispered to me that there had been a plan
afoot for Lord Beaverbrook in that case to become
Prime Minister; for Lady Diana Cooper to be Mistress
of the Robes, next to the Queen; and for Duff-Cooper
to be the Lord Chamberlain.

Then, as the heralds trumpeted, the Dukes of
Gloucester and Kent, in their robes still more gorgeous
than any we had seen, took their seats in front of the
peers. Shortly another fanfare and a burst of organ
music. The King and Queen are moving up the aisle,
and the Westminster choir sings the Psalm: "I was glad

when they said unto me, Let us go into the house of the Lord." The Queen is in the lead, with six peeresses carrying her train. Then the King, with nine peers and pages carrying his still longer train. The King and Queen kneel and pray, alone—before the great golden altar.

The Archbishop of Canterbury, accompanied by the Lord Chancellor, speaks first to those who are in the eastern end of the Abbey, then to those at the south, at the west, and to us at the north. Each time he says: "Sirs, I here present unto you King George, your undoubted King." And each time the shout went up: "God save King George!"

Then followed the hour-long ritual, the coronation oath, the anointing, and the crowning of both the King and Queen. Powerful concealed lights illuminated the scene around the altar, the lights for the hidden cameramen who were making the Coronation motion pictures. These lights, falling on the royal jewels, and all the glitter and gold, almost blinded us.

In many years of traveling about the world, I have witnessed pageants in many lands, including dazzling durbars of India. But none could compare with the dignity and splendor of this coronation pageant at Westminster Abbey.

In the gallery just below us sat one of the most distinguished men of India, a stately Parsee dignitary from Bombay. The Parsee kept his Zoroastrian headdress on most of the time, as is the custom of the Parsees. Like so many other Easterners, when indoors they take off their shoes and keep on their hats. His was tall, like a stovepipe. But now and then this fire-worshiper from Hindustan would take his hat off and hold it in his lap—revealing an egg-shaped head, utterly bald.

A resplendent British nobleman beside me stood up for a better view. The Archbishop of Canterbury was in the midst of the impressive anointing ceremony. Holding the golden ampulla and pouring oil from it, His Grace said to the King: "Be thy head anointed with holy oil—as Solomon was anointed king by Zadok the priest." His Lordship, standing beside me, was wearing his sword, and, turning to whisper to me, he swung his sword around, raking the scabbard right across the Parsee's bald head. Whereupon the Parsee uttered words of wrath.

We all had books in our laps—each of us had been given a bound volume entitled, *The Form and Order of the Service That Is to Be Performed and the Ceremonies That Are to Be Observed in the Coronation*. Only a few minutes after His Lordship had apologized for raking the Parsee's bald head with the sword, he stood up again. The Archbishop of Canterbury was handing the golden scepter to George VI, saying as he did so: "Receive the Rod of Equity and Mercy. . . . Be so merciful that you be not too remiss." At that moment His Lordship's bound book of the service slipped from under his arm and crashed down on the bald Parsee head. Whereupon the follower of Zoroaster from Bombay rose out of his seat, rubbed his head and muttered remarks which were not at all similar to the words which His Grace the Archbishop was uttering to the King just below us.

Altogether the ceremony went off faultlessly—except for one aged dignitary who became wound up in his robes and was said to have dislocated his shoulder when he approached the throne to pay homage and kiss the King.

There were no gross mishaps such as figured in coronations of the past. Nothing like the scene of 871 years ago when William the Conqueror was crowned. Then the uproar inside the Abbey made the Norman soldiers outside think there was a Saxon uprising. Whereupon they fell upon and massacred all Saxons who were near.

Nor was there confusion like that at the coronation of George III, when the monarch didn't know when to put on his crown and asked the Archbishop, who asked the Bishop of Rochester, who asked somebody else, and so on, and then didn't find out. At that same coronation of George III, dignitaries of the realm fell to fighting for precedence. The Deputy Earl Marshal lost the sword of state and had to borrow a saber to take its place. Somebody forgot the royal canopy, and there were no chairs for the King and Queen. Most shocking of all, the Lord High Steward's horse became confused and backed into the throne.

No, nothing like that at the coronation of George VI. They tell me it was the most perfect, the most spectacular and impressive, in all British history.

VII

The Wedding at Cande

The marriage in exile of the ex-king and the lady from Baltimore, now the Duke and Duchess of Windsor, maintained the standards of the dramatic, not without a touch of the comic that had distinguished the royal romance from the beginning. He had renounced a throne to gain a wife, and gain a wife he did—with an emphatic abundance of ritual.

The great salon in the Château de Cande was aglow with flowers. No wedding ceremony had ever been more beautifully arranged. Everything was flowers, the blooms and blossoms of Touraine. Accord-

126

ing to familiar custom in France, it was a double marriage—civil and religious.

The civil rite was performed first, by the local mayor. It was strictly the routine, according to the book—the law book, the legal formalities prescribed by French law. And this was somewhat in contrast to the flame of lofty romance of a king who had abandoned his throne for the woman he loved.

Monsieur Mercier, a typical French provincial mayor, began by reciting the following: "Conforming to the requirements of the law I will read you Chapter Six of the Civil Code on the respective rights and duties of a married couple." With that highly sentimental beginning, the mayor read Articles Two Hundred Twelve, Thirteen, Fourteen and Fifteen of Chapter Six. One of the articles went this way: "The wife must live with her husband and must follow him to whatever place he deems proper as a residence. The husband must receive her and furnish her with the necessities of life according to his facilities and position."

Not such exalted romance that. But then the business of supporting a wife is not neglected in the French marriage ceremony. The French are so practical.

Then Mayor Mercier led the couple through the formalities of taking their vows, after which he made the culminating pronouncement: "In the name of the law, I declare you united in the bonds of matrimony."

So they were married, according to the civil rite of France. They now stood, Duke and Duchess of Windsor, His Royal Highness and Her Grace. Wally was not granted royal rank equivalent to that of her husband. He was a royal duke, she just a duchess.

Don't think the French mayor was through. Not at all. The custom of France permits the official that performs the marriage to deliver an address, make a speech, to the newly wedded couple. Mayor Mercier was determined not to neglect the opportunity. This renowned marriage which had come his way had made him suddenly famous—a world figure. He was basking in historic limelight.

Every provincial French mayor loves to make a speech, like every other kind of mayor, and here was the opportunity of a lifetime for Mayor Mercier and his sonorous French eloquence. People attached to the Duke of Windsor had gone to the mayor with delicate hints and tactful suggestions—not to make his address too long. Because French mayors are also known for their long-winded speeches. The mayor agreed that he would not speak for two or three hours. No, his oration was not that long, but it was long enough, and he made up for his comparative brevity with flights of oratory.

Let me repeat one of his oratorical flights, which really hit the ceiling of French eloquence. Addressing the Duke and Duchess, the mayor cried: "This famous love, which innumerable hearts secretly celebrate today, represents France, which has always been attracted by gallant disinterestedness and bold behavior inspired by the heart."

The mayor was magnificent as he said this, because the French are really enthusiastic about "the bold be-

havior inspired by the heart." The English are a little
different.

The mayor, amid his rolling phrases and romantic
fervor, could not resist a little local town boosting,
scenery selling, with an eye to the tourists. He wove
the boosting in rather neatly. "By one of those caprices
of destiny," he cried with ecstasy, "it is under the blue
sky of France, on the bank of our charming river here,
that one of the most moving of ideals is being achieved."
Our own American chambers of commerce don't usually get it in that smoothly.

The mayor's peroration soared to the sky and then
hit that noble theme of international friendship: "I
salute the prince," he declaimed, "the prince who was
sovereign of a friendly country, and the lady he has
chosen from a country to which France is attached
by the same close ties." So the mayor closed on a note
of French, British and American alliance—a comfortable thought in France, the international situation
being what it was.

After the civil rite of France came the religious
service of the Church of England, and there at once
the mood of the occasion deepened into grandeur. A
Yorkshire clergyman, the Vicar of Darlington, the poor
man's parson, was defying his church and ecclesiastical
superiors by giving religious marriage to the exiled
English king and the twice-divorced American woman.
He was doing it without permission. He was taking
his clerical life in his hands.

Back in England they were angry about the Vicar's
temerity. His immediate pastoral superior had tele-

graphed, reproving him. The council and trustees of his church had met and decreed their disapproval. His bishop had disclaimed his action. The Archbishop of Canterbury was indignant because of this breach of discipline. But meanwhile in England other voices were raised saying other things—complaints against the Church of England for its unrelenting hostility toward this bridegroom and bride. There were expressions of public approval for the obscure clergyman who was defying that unrelenting hostility.

What would be the destiny of the poor man's parson? Would he be punished, would his clerical career be ruined by what he was about to do? Such was the mood and depth of drama, as the Reverend R. Ander-son Jardine read those all-familiar phrases: "Dearly beloved, we are gathered together here in the sight of God to join this man and this woman in holy matri-mony, which is an honorable estate." The solemnity was overwhelming. The beauty was disturbing—after the French civil code and the eloquence of the mayor.

The middle-aged clergyman intoned the promise: "Wilt thou take this woman as thy wedded wife, to live together after God's ordinance in the holy state of matrimony?" He read the vow with a grave, earnest voice.

Edward's voice was vibrant and thrilling as he pro-nounced: "I will."

Then came the vow of the Duchess of Windsor. She listened with tears in her eyes as the promise was re-cited to her and as she gave the promise, "I will."

It was a thing of solemn beauty—that Church of

England marriage service. But did it count? There were hints from England that the Reverend Jardine had no canonical right to perform a marriage without permission outside of his parish, therefore the wedding ritual was void. This was quite academic. For Edward and Wally were married, were the Duke and Duchess of Windsor, when the French mayor got through with his ritual. They were man and wife before the Church of England ceremony began. So, was the reality of the occasion in the French civil code and the mayor's eloquence? And was there only unreality in the affecting beauty that followed? Moody questions to be asked about the wedding that consummated the royal romance.

VIII

Love Affairs of State

Romance always has a fillip of added interest when it has to do with personages lofty in royalty or government. When a swain of kingly family says: "Will you be mine?" it's headline copy. When sentimental raptures come to the ménage of a Chief of State, we pause with attention. So let's scan some sundry instances of royal and governmental heart throbs.

The news told how along the valley of the Danube a special train rolled under heavy guard toward Switzerland. Aboard it was ex-King Carol of

Rumania going into exile with the great love of his life, Magda Lupescu, daughter of a Jewish junk dealer from Budapest.

From Dresden in Germany toward Bucharest rolled another special train. That one carried a sad, dark-haired, dignified lady, ex-Queen Helen of Rumania, Carol's divorced wife, returning to join her young son, Michael, from whom she had been parted so long. Somewhere in the valley of the Danube those two trains may have passed each other—the deserted, neglected ex-queen and the junk dealer's daughter who stole her king away from her.

It was interesting to read the telegram with which Dictator Antonescu addressed Queen Helen: "I beg you to take your place alongside your son to complete his education for the happiness of all Rumania, and end all the suffering to which Your Majesty has been subjected." So she returned, alone but in triumph, to the capital that she once had left in grief and humiliation.

Twice within a period of three years a reigning sovereign had gone into exile with the woman he loved. First, Edward VIII, sovereign to the British Empire. Next his second cousin, Carol of Rumania. But there was one large difference between the two cousins. For ten years Carol had not only the woman he loved but his crown as well. For ten years he played a dangerous, crafty and successful game. He might still have retained both, sitting firmly on the Hohenzollern throne in Rumania, but for the overwhelming sweep of Nazi aggression. Hostile pro-Nazi crowds outside the royal palace focused part of their anger on Magda Lupescu. But Hitler would have toppled Carol over, Magda or no Magda.

There were tears in Carol's eyes when he finally yielded, and abdicated. The time was dawn. All night the dictator, Antonescu, brought argument after argument to bear upon the King. It took all night to convince him that the Army upon whom he relied did not want him any more. Two of his prime ministers had been assassinated by the Fascist Iron Guard, and Carol had punished the murderers relentlessly. Now, when he realized the Army was against him, he gave up.

Carol of Rumania's reign was over, and it seemed likely that his exile would not be as gay as the previous one. That time he enjoyed the flesh pots of life in Paris with Magda at his side. Now Magda was still at his side, a plump and aging Magda, but none of the flesh pots of Paris. It was even a guess how well he was financed. The crowds that yelled outside his palace gates shouted: "Away with Carol!" And they also shouted: "But don't let him take the money."

The cabled news from wartime London told what a girl was planning to do that night. She intended to go to the movies—alone, all by herself, no boy friend in tow. She said she would be home by nine-thirty, and be mighty prompt about it, to be there when the telephone rang. She would be sitting, waiting for the telephone call.

All of which might have seemed to be rather girlish and trivial for a London news bulletin in wartime—not, however, when we observed the one from whom the girl expected the telephone call—Gerald Lascelles, son of the Earl of Harewood. His mother was the sister of King George. So he was the nephew of the sovereign of Great Britain, and was in fact in line of succession to the British throne—tenth in line. His telephone call tonight was part of a story of romance—and royal romance always was a headline.

But not so much of a headline in England, where one newspaper printed the story and then quickly withdrew it—by request. It told that the nephew of the King, who was eighteen years old, had become engaged to the seventeen-year-old daughter of a British Army lieutenant. She was a commoner—he royalty.

American newspaper correspondents in London procured an account of the young romance. Gerald Lascelles and June Morris met on a bus. That was related by the girl's mother. "June and Gerald really did meet on top of a bus," said Mrs. Morris. "It was a case of love at first sight, because June did not know who Gerald was." June found that out later.

She introduced Gerald to other girls, and one was quoted as saying, "He is a handsome fellow, and a good pick for any girl." As why wouldn't he be—nephew of the King, and tenth in line of succession to the throne of England.

After falling in love at first sight, the young couple went around together constantly—to movies, dances, theaters. The London story specified that they went always by bus, the way they had met. Gerald called at June's home three times a week, and then they became engaged.

They knew they could not be legally married without special permission. But they were determined. June's mother told how Gerald said: "I am quite prepared to go through with this, and leave the country if necessary."

She was a war worker in a canteen, and he was being called into the Army. So he went away. But he telephoned her every evening, and June made sure to be home at the time to receive the call from him.

Here is a royal romance that offers an interesting hint or two. If you're bashful about proposing marriage to your best girl, have her give you a manicure. Or maybe a shampoo would make it still easier. While she douses your head with suds, that's the time to utter the words, "Will you be mine?"

How Prince George of England proposed to Princess Marina of Greece was illuminated with full details. The Princess herself told what happened. The royal son of Their Majesties, King George and Queen Mary, glanced at his fingernails.

"Pretty bad, I'll have to get a manicure," observed His Royal Highness.

"Couldn't I do it for you?" asked Her Royal Highness.

In no time she had a bowl of soapy water, a nail

file and an orange stick. The first hand was about finished when His Royal Highness asked: "How would you like to have the King and Queen of England for your father-in-law and mother-in-law?"

Her Royal Highness answered, "O-o-oh, I'd love it!"

That's the way it was arranged between Their Royal Highnesses. The romantic manicuring hit the nail on the head, a cuticle way of proposing. The royal precedent might set a new fashion, marriage by manicure, or popping the question while getting a shampoo—or suppose your best girl happened to be a chiropodist?

There was one royal wedding of recent years that might well have been called a sports marriage. The bridegroom of Crown Princess Juliana of Holland, who one day would be the ruling queen, had to fit a definite pattern—for reasons of state. But then personal inclinations play a part in many matches, even in royal nuptials. It's a good thing for a bridegroom and bride to have similar tastes. In this case the bride was much inclined toward outdoor sports—skating and tennis. As a little girl she became an adept at flashing the gliding blades on the Dutch ice—racing by the windmills. She thought so much of tennis as to have received earnest instructions from some of the best racquet experts in her mother's kingdom.

The theme of skating tied nicely with the report that Princess Juliana met her bridegroom at the Olympic winter games. There they became acquainted, and presumably she was courted while watching the skiing, bob-sledding and skating. Lovers on ice.

The theme of tennis led to matters more solemn and royal. The first thing that reasons of state demanded in cutting the pattern for Juliana's bridegroom was that he must be of royal blood. There was talk that the Princess felt romantic inclinations toward a young nobleman of the Netherlands. He was an aristocrat, but not royal, so the romance had to die. There was talk of a possible alliance between Juliana and a Swedish royal prince. That would have been all right, according to reasons of state—but the bridegroom turned out to be somebody else. His lineage was just as royal, and moreover it tied to tennis.

Prince Bernhard Leopold Frederic Jules Curt Charles Godfrey Peter von Lippe was a nephew of Prince Leopold IV, who was ruler of the principality of Lippe until the German revolution tossed out the princelings. So Prince Bernhard, et cetera, et cetera, came from an ancient clan that went back to the twelfth century. His mother was of the German von Cramm family, the most notable present-day representative of which was Baron von Cramm, the tennis player. He was the German racquet champ, and ranked at the top with the first half-dozen players on the international list—he did until he disappeared in an unsavory scandal.

The reasons of state went on to specify that the prince consort of the future queen of Holland must be a Protestant. That was natural, since Holland was ruled by the House of Orange. You can ask any Irish-

man what "Orange" means. Moreover, the prince consort must not be in line of succession to any European
throne, because Holland didn't want to be dynastically
hitched with any other kingdom. Prince Bernhard and
so on and so on von Lippe fitted the bill to perfection.
And, incidentally, by the way, the Princess was in love
with him.

I hope I have made clear by this time that Princess
Juliana, daughter of Queen Wilhelmina, was both
athletic and royal. In addition she was learned. At the
University of Leyden she won an honorary Doctorate
of Laws. She sat at the feet of the great Snouck Hur-
gronje, authority on Moslem law. She was a deep student of Latin, history, geography, political economy,
art, singing, the violin and seven languages. What
could you add to that?

We could add this, a tribute to the placid good
nature of the sturdy Princess. She was dancing once
when she overheard a man making a remark in French.
French was one of those seven languages. Too bad she
had learned it, because the Frenchman was speaking
about the extremities on which the Princess was dancing. "Voilà!" exclaimed the astonished Frenchman.
"Look at that pair of pillars!"

Juliana turned to him with gently smiling eyes and
replied in perfect French: "They have to be big. Some
day they'll be the pillars of state." So, in addition to
her other qualifications, the gracious Princess Juliana
of Holland had a sense of humor.

Once more the fate of the mountains befell the royal family of Belgium. The year before it was the mountaineer king, Albert, killed while climbing a peak. Now Queen Astrid, come to an untimely end while motoring through the mountains. The young royal couple loved lofty summits, just as King Albert did. The mountains were the fascination of Belgian royalty—also the doom.

They were driving among the towering Swiss Alps on the lovely shore of Lake Lucerne. King Leopold was at the wheel. His chauffeur was sitting beside him in the front seat. Queen Astrid was in the back seat. They were going fifty miles an hour. The King took his eyes off the road to glance at a road map. At that moment somehow the car swung off and hit the curb at the side of the road, careened and smashed into a tree, then bounced off into the shallow waters of the lake.

Queen Astrid was hurled out of the car, and struck the tree. The King was thrown clear, cut and bruised, but not badly hurt. The chauffeur was critically injured. The young husband hurried to his wife, and picked her up. She lived bare seconds, died in his arms.

Astrid was Princess of Sweden, daughter of Prince Charles and Princess Ingeborg. She was a niece of the Swedish King. She grew up in the stately dignity of royal tradition, and made her first formal public appearance when she was thirteen, at a Red Cross fête. Then it was noticed how lovely she was, with a dark-haired grace and charm. As she became a young woman, they saw how devoted she was to winter sports, games in the snow and ice. The Swedes liked her all the better for that. They called her the "Snow Princess." In the royalty of Europe there was none more enchanting than the young, good-looking Snow Princess.

In 1925 the Swedish court received a visit of state from the then Queen of Belgium and her young son Leopold. Inevitably there was a meeting of the Belgian Crown Prince and the Swedish Snow Princess, and they saw a good deal of each other. She was then twenty, he was twenty-three. That began a romance which culminated in marriage—and three children, a girl and two boys.

The tragedy of King Albert in the mountains made Astrid a queen. Then once more in the mountains—the end of the Snow Princess.

There was sadness in Vienna because an old, old woman was no more. There was mourning in the vicinity of Schoenbrunn Palace, near which she lived—mourning especially among the beggars. For that old, old woman many years before had been a friend of the Emperor, the stately monarch who reigned in Schoenbrunn Palace. And she was a bene-factress of beggars, giving every one she met a bright smile and a bright silver coin.

She was known to history as Frau Kathleen von Kiss-Schratt. To Vienna she was known as Kathi. For thirty years she was the friend and confidante of the Emperor Francis Joseph, monarch of the Austro-Hungarian Empire. She was smiles and laughter to that stony, stern and tragic sovereign. She was witty, clever, chatty, entertaining. She kept the Emperor amused—she also kept him informed and advised, with the information that comes in gossip and lively banter, the advice that comes from a shrewd feminine judgment of persons and events.

An Austrian historian, in writing the life of Francis Joseph, had this to say of Kathi, the monarch's friend: "She was the link between the Emperor and the outer world. She was his newspaper. From her he learned more than from all his ministers put together."

They called her the "uncrowned empress," for uncrowned she was. The Emperor's son Rudolf was the victim of a romance with a girl he could not marry because she was not of royal blood. Rudolf and his beauty were killed in a mysterious tragedy. Then there was the Emperor's kinsman, the Archduke who married a woman of common rank, renounced his royal rights —and sailed away to vanish in a mystery of the sea. The imperial Hapsburgs did not marry commoners.

Somber Francis Joseph was no philanderer. He was a paragon of methodical and steady-going life. He was devoted to his Empress, the mad, tragic Elizabeth. She led a distracted career of fantastic adventures and travels—finally to perish by the hand of an anarchist assassin. It was the imperial Elizabeth who introduced to her Emperor husband the beautiful young actress of the Vienna stage, Kathi Schratt. Elizabeth encour-

142

aged Francis Joseph to seek solace in the society of Kathi.

Thereafter for long years their companionship was constant—the Emperor and the uncrowned empress. Kathi was no La Pompadour or Du Barry, in that she never sought to use her position to wield political power. She employed her influence over the Emperor to no other purpose than small deeds of kindliness and charity. Vienna grew to love the uncrowned empress—that gay Vienna of the old times which could waltz and smile its tolerance.

After the death of Francis Joseph, Kathi, an old woman, lived in retirement, giving charity to beggars and talking wistfully of the good old days. It was her constant byword, referring back to the joyful time when she was young and beautiful and when her Emperor was at the height of his glory. She saw the downfall of the Austro-Hungarian Empire—and sighed for the good old days.

When she was told that the Nazi Germans had taken Austria, she gaped in amazement and exclaimed, "Ah, for the good old days!"

She died at eighty-seven, asking for no better heaven than something like those good old days.

A radio listener of Springfield, Massachusetts, sent me a clipping from a Springfield paper telling the story of romance between an American woman and a king—and their marriage. Not a lady from Baltimore, but a girl from Springfield. Not a king of England, but a king of Portugal.

Back in the 1840's, a Swiss tailor and his family emigrated to America and settled down in Springfield, Massachusetts. He opened a tailoring shop there. His eldest daughter, Elise, sang in the choir of the North Church. The beauty of her voice was the sensation of the town. She studied for opera, went to Europe and became a renowned prima donna.

In due time Elise Hensler, the girl from Springfield, opened a brilliant operatic season at Lisbon, in the opera "La Somnambula." She sang divinely. The Portuguese ruling family sat in the royal box and acclaimed her with enthusiasm—especially the King. He fell in love with her then and there, love at first sight. He got an introduction to her, and it wasn't long before he proposed marriage. She accepted—and became the King's wife in June, 1852. She even became queen. They had no great constitutional scruples about that in Portugal. The girl from Springfield became Countess of Elda—consort to His Majesty, King Ferdinand of Portugal.

One of the most amazing legal cases in the history of the courts was decided by a judge in Paris, after dragging along for sixty years. It was a suit against the Swiss city of Geneva for a legacy of a hundred million dollars.

It all went back to royal affairs at the court of England, back to 1825, when George IV was on the throne. In that year a nephew of the king arrived from Germany. The Georges of the Hanoverian dynasty were Germans, and the king's nephew was the Duke of Brunswick. He was a young man, only twenty-nine, and at the British court he fell deeply in love with the beautiful Lady Charlotte Colville. As she was not of royal blood, he couldn't marry her. He took her back to Brunswick and settled her at the castle of Wessenden. The following year a daughter was born. The Duke issued letters patent, recognizing the child as his own and conferring on her the title of Countess of Colmar.

Two years later, there was a quarrel between the Duke and Lady Charlotte Colville. She returned to England. The child remained with the Duke. Several years after that a revolution in Brunswick drove the Duke from his throne. He went to Paris. The little Countess of Colmar went with him. In his Parisian exile he became famous as an eccentric. He retained his vast private fortune, and money makes eccentricity more eccentric. For years he was one of the bizarre characters of the city that understood and tolerated.

When the Countess of Colmar was sixteen the event occurred that led to all the future legal proceedings. The girl became a Catholic. The Duke was furious. He packed her off to London, trying to make her change her mind. He stopped her allowance, putting pressure on her. But she met a young French nobleman, Count Ulrich de Civry, and married him. And that ended the eccentric Duke's right to influence his daughter on the subject of religion. He never forgave her.

He died in 1873, leaving a will which bequeathed all of his immense estate to the city of Geneva, on condition that the authorities of Geneva have his body petrified. He himself had invented a way to do the petrifying. And the city was to place him in a magnificent mausoleum. The Count de Civry and his Countess challenged the will, claiming that the Duke was not in his right mind when he made the strange testament and that they were the legal heirs. The city of Geneva denied this, and the case went dragging through the French courts.

One part of the evidence concerned documents in that august sanctuary, the British Museum, letters patent concerning the Countess of Colmar's birth. The originals had burned in the turmoil of the Brunswick revolution, which had overthrown the Duke. Copies had been put on record in London—so claimed Count de Civry. But the city of Geneva protested that these copies in the British Museum were forgeries. The city further claimed that the royal birth records of Brunswick had been falsified.

The case dragged on for sixty years, and when finally decided the city of Geneva won. The claim, based on an old romantic story, was denied.

❧

Boris, King of Andorra, was trying to establish his royal rights—with the aid of an American girl friend, he said. The tiny semi-independent nation in the Pyrenees had an idea that it might become a monarchy, and various aspirants appeared, seeking to be king.

A Chicago millionaire offered to buy the throne of Andorra. The Andorrans refused. Some said it was because the Chicago price was too low. Boris didn't offer any money for the throne—he didn't seem to have any money. He simply moved in and proclaimed himself king. But he wasn't even king for a day. His subjects refused to pay homage, and he was put in jail—which distinctly was not homage.

The Spanish police had him in jail at Barcelona, and conducted an inquiry to find out who he really was. Boris was perfectly willing to tell them, but they wanted some proof—like a birth certificate, an affidavit by his parents, and a line or two out of the old family Bible. He talked a dozen languages and identified himself in each one, but the police didn't believe him in any one of them.

He claimed to be the Baron of Skoseyreff and Count of Orange. Instead of "Count," the police said "no account." Instead of "Orange," they said "lemon." He explained that he was of Dutch descent, but the Catalonian cops thought he was Polish. He added that he was broke, and they believed that all right.

King Boris proclaimed that he was waiting for an American girl friend to send him some cash. Maybe so. Those benevolent American girl friends in Europe were an old stand-by for all sorts of gigolos. American womanhood, when decorated with a bankroll, inspired faith and hope, and supplied the charity. The man who would be king declared that his feminine financial backer had promised to send him the money to raise reinforcements to conquer his kingdom.

He warned darkly that any attempt to deprive him of his royal crown would result in a great war in the Mediterranean. Adjusting a monocle in his eye, he stated that three of the world's greatest powers were ready to come to his rescue and defend his claims. Two of these great powers were European. The third was the United States. America would rush to his aid— the girl friend presumably would see to that. Which made the comedy complete to the last giggle, with visions of the American fleet steaming in warlike array to put King Boris the First of Andorra on his Pyrenean throne. He had a lot of confidence in America—the American government and that American girl friend.

Amid ominous news of rioting, bloodshed and possible political upheaval in Paris, came word of the shooting of a high dignitary, a nobleman of lofty lineage—shot by a woman. "A grave political crime," so the wires flashed. Then we heard that it was what the French so aptly call a crime of passion. In the crisis of rioting and national peril, the sensation was heart throbs and bullets. The exquisite touch— Vive la France!

The notables mentioned were lofty indeed: the victim of the shooting, Count Charles de Chambrun, a statesman of France, recently French ambassador to Rome, a descendant of Lafayette; his wife, with him at the time, the Princess Murat, descendant of Napoleon's famous Marshal. As a descendant of Lafayette, the Count was a hereditary American citizen, and he had distinguished American family connections—his sister-in-law, a sister of the late Nicholas Longworth, Speaker of our own House of Representatives and husband of Princess Alice of the Roosevelt clan, daughter of the mighty Teddy.

The lady with the pistol was Madame de Fontanges, a French journalist, daughter of a famous woman artist. She was a beautiful flashing brunette, this Madame de Fontanges. She was an actress who had starred in several Parisian plays and then had turned to newspaper writing. Madame used a small pistol. Anything so bulky as a forty-five would no doubt have been too crude and ungraceful for her elegant hands. So she fired with a dainty pistollet, which, moreover, jammed after the first shot. In addition, she fired at the Count's heart, and hit him in the knee.

"I am sorry," Madame cried later, "sorry that I did not kill him. I regret the pistol jammed. For he ruined the great love of my life."

With whom was she in love? That was the delicate question.

"He is such a high personage," exclaimed Madame, "that I cannot mention his name. But he is my great love."

She explained that her grand passion was thwarted by Count de Chambrun, when he was Ambassador to

149

Rome. She confided to him the secret of her heart, which he basely told to many people and made it public gossip. One can picture the Count relating the story over a bottle of Chambertin with light laughter and flashes of French wit. Anyway, it blighted the romance of Madame. She had to leave Italy, and returned to France, far from the man whom she adored.

The Paris police investigated Madame's apartment, and there they found the walls literally covered with photographs, portraits of one man—Mussolini. On the north wall were a dozen or so pictures of the Duce—scowling. On the south wall were a dozen more of the same—scowling. And similarly on the east and west walls—Madame's living room filled with the scowls of Mussolini. The French police reasoned shrewdly. Could it be that this was her great love—Mussolini? So that was why the descendant of Lafayette got shot.

It was recalled that while in Rome Madame, as a journalist, had several long interviews with the Duce. These had appeared in the French newspapers. An inquiry flashed to Rome brought back the statement that while in Italy Madame had pestered certain high officials—who were left unnamed. Reporters quizzed Madame's lawyer, saying they had information that she was a friend of Mussolini. Whereupon the lawyer threw up his hands and cried, "Don't quote me mentioning his name!" All this made the love shooting an international affair, especially when the case came before the judge, for a preliminary hearing, and Madame cried with ardor—it was Mussolini.

The name of still another celebrity was mentioned.

Testifying in court, Madame dragged in no less a magnifico than a former Premier of France, Monsieur Joseph Paul-Boncour. He used to be her friend, said Madame de Fontanges. A dear friend, she added. But, alas, he turned against her. He did her out of a job she had at Geneva, a job reporting a meeting of the League of Nations. Later when Count de Chambrun, French ambassador to Rome, interfered in her Roman romance, he did so at the insistence of the former Premier of France, His Excellency Paul-Boncour.

She found herself unable to see the Duce any longer, Madame said, and it broke her heart. She felt so badly that she took an overdose of a sleeping powder. She was taken to a hospital in Rome and there the Duce's secretary visited her every day. After she was well enough to leave the hospital and go to a hotel, Mussolini's secretary continued to call on her every day. These visits were consoling for a while. That is, until the last one. On that fatal day she learned the news that she must leave Italy. She made no fuss about it, and upon her departure was given an envelope by a Fascist officer of state. In that envelope was the handsome sum of one thousand, three hundred and fifty dollars.

After being expelled from Italy she continued to write to the Duce, but got no reply. Then she learned that Mussolini had gone to Libya. That, she said, made her desperate. She bought the revolver and tried to make a date with the Count de Chambrun by telephone, using a phony name. The ruse did not succeed. Later she learned that he was going to Brussels and what train he was to take. And so she met him at the station, and shot him.

After the hearing, the lady was taken to the hospital, suffering severely from bronchitis—after talking so much.

The climax of the case produced a rich coincidence. It was Mussolini's birthday. He was fifty-four. He had a great celebration at a resort on the Adriatic—the kind of celebration the Duce liked, a review of warships. There was also a sort of Mussolini celebration in Paris. On the Duce's birthday Madame de Fontages was brought to trial. She faced the court, evidence was given, and a verdict was handed down.

The legal proceedings were surrounded by guarded secrecy, because it was feared that Madame might talk so loudly and volubly about Mussolini and his love for her as to provoke an international crisis. But enough got out to fill in the picture with some rosy details.

Elinor Glyn limited ecstasy to three weeks, but Madame's Roman idyl sighed and languished for three months. The evidence that she presented included her diary full of purple descriptions and three hundred photographs of Mussolini, some of them supposedly signed by him with tender salutations. He'd hardly have autographed all three hundred with lovelorn epithets. That would have been laborious even for a hard-working dictator.

Madame enriched the picture of how her romance was shattered through the machinations of Count de Chambrun, descendant of Lafayette and French ambassador to Italy. The Count, she claimed, whispered poisonous words about her to Mussolini, and destroyed the Duce's love for her. Then the descendant of La-fayette, in interviews with her, kissed and caressed her. While blighting her great love, he tried to give her another to take its place.

The verdict handed down by the court had interest-ing implications. The defendant was on trial for hav-ing shot the Count de Chambrun, and nobody denied she had done just that. So she was found guilty. What was the penalty? A year in jail—but the sentence was suspended, which made it not even ten minutes in jail. And Madame was fined a hundred francs. With the exchange what it was, that came to thirty-seven dollars and a half. That much for shooting the former ambassador and descendant of Lafayette. The Count de Chambrun in the court proceedings demanded damages for having been shot—which seemed fair enough. The court awarded him damages—one franc, which was not quite four cents.

I don't know how to philosophize on this French verdict, but I suppose the gentleness of the punish-ment inflicted on Madame would indicate the follow-ing: that the court believed her story of the Mussolini romance was true; and that she was more or less justi-fied in starting to shoot when it was broken off—which I take to have been a compliment to Mussolini.

The case had a headline epilogue on our side of the ocean, and this brought laurels not to any of those statesmen of Europe, but to our own Bureau of Immi-gration. Madame de Fontanges decided to visit the

United States, sailed to our shores, and was held at Ellis Island. What to do with her?

Suppose the Immigration Bureau had admitted Madame into this country of ours, had given her a cordial welcome—might that not have offended the Count de Chambrun, a descendant of Lafayette? He might have cried: "Lafayette, they are not here!"

But suppose they had excluded Madame, and deported her? That would have had a delicate point. Because the usual reason for deporting a fair lady is moral turpitude. If they had sent away Madame because of moral turpitude—would that not have been an affirmation of her story about Mussolini? By finding her guilty, we would also have found the Duce guilty. And that would have been a high affair of state—convicting the black-shirt dictator *in absentia* of moral turpitude. Of course, Mussolini and the Italians were not famous for drawing such a fine Puritanical line. They called moral turpitude *l'amore,* which sounds more romantic. Just the same, our wise men of immigration needed the sharpest of wit in putting the United States of America on record in the case of Madame's alleged unforgettable three months with the Duce in Rome. And they needed the subtlest of wit.

That's exactly what they displayed. After much speculation Rudolph Riner, Commissioner of Immigration at Ellis Island, announced that Madame de Fontanges would be deported. On what grounds? Why, moral turpitude. But what kind? Moral turpitude is like charity, it covers a multitude of sins. It could include not only unforgettable months, but also shooting. Our sagacious immigration men carefully avoided touching upon the romantic and perilous theme of Madame and Mussolini. They merely cited the fact, undisputed and quite safe, that Madame shot the descendant of Lafayette in the knee and right then was under a suspended sentence of one year handed down by the French courts. The official decision read: ". . . because of the commission of a crime involving moral turpitude, to wit, assault with a dangerous weapon." Now if that wasn't witty, I'm the Duce!

❦

At Washington, D. C., a lawsuit was filed, and amid all the legal verbiage of whereas and wherefore, allege and affirm, one of the strangest stories is told. It was a tale of government intrigue in Latin America, a death threat issued by the President of Peru to an American. This followed a forced marriage. Lewis Clarkson asked the annulment of his legal union to a lady of Peru. Clarkson was an American businessman who formerly lived and transacted commerce in Peru. The Señora was described as a mystery woman of deep, dark secrets.

The legal documents filed in Washington related how one day twelve years before, in the old stately city of Lima, Clarkson was summoned to the palace of President Leguia. There, after the exchange of compliments, the President spoke up and asked Clarkson to marry the mysterious Señora.

Clárkson was astounded. He knew the Señora, had met her a year before. Moreover, he had heard a great deal about her. The legal papers described her as follows: "A person of bad reputation commonly known to be involved in Peruvian political intrigues and to be supported by various prominent government officials, including the President of the Republic." Such was the bride the American businessman was asked to take, asked by the President of Peru.

He said, "No." He repeated, "No." Leguia, the President, replied—that he'd better, or there might be an accidental shooting, some mishap of gunfire, and Clarkson would be the victim.

The marriage occurred shortly afterward, when four presidential secret service men came to Clarkson's home, and escorted him to the church. They were escorts who seemed quite likely to put into effect the presidential alternative—a wedding or an accidental shooting.

The marriage, under such circumstances, was hardly what you'd call a success, not one of those lifelong unions of bliss. Clarkson and his bride saw the last of each other several months later. They went their separate ways, and in 1928 Clarkson heard that the Señora had died. Two years after that things in Peru blew up with a revolution, and President Leguia was deposed. More recently, Clarkson discovered that the rumor of the Señora's death was false—she was very much alive. Whereupon he asked the District of Columbia courts to dissolve what may well be called a Peruvian shotgun wedding.

IX

Exotic Romance of State

Nuptial proceedings in the realm of royalty and rulers achieve the height of flamboyance when they occur in places distant and different from ours. We think of the Orient and tropical isles, with their tribes and principalities, as traditional scenes of dramatics colorful and strange—and what could be more so than nuptial romance and exotic potentates?

The Japs, in robbing China of spacious Manchuria, did not neglect to employ matrimony as an instrument of international banditry. To the brutalities of war they added wedding bells, orange blossoms and bridal veil. Or rather, the cherry dance, a Shinto melody, the waving of laurel branches and nine cups of wine. The day chosen for the ceremony was a sign of how much a matter of state the wedding was. Japanese national egotism, nourished by freakish and megalomaniac superstitions, is reflected in the feast in commemoration of the death of Emperor Jimmu. He, so their arrogant legend relates, was the first mortal ruler of Nippon. Before him the emperors were divinities. Jimmu, the first royal mortal, was the fifth descendant of the sun goddess—she Japan's first sovereign. No day more fitting could be selected for a wedding designed to promote the feast of Japanese flagrant aggression that was to lead to world-wide war.

The bride was Hiroko Saga, granddaughter of the Marquis of Saga, one of Japan's lordliest nobles. The groom was Cavalry Lieutenant Tu Chieh. He was the brother of the Emperor Kang-Teh of Manchukuo, Japan's puppet state. Kang-Teh had no children, so the bridegroom stood as the next heir to the throne of the Manchus. The marriage was intended to strengthen the bonds between the Tokyo government and the fraudulent kingdom it set up in conquered Manchuria.

The nuptial ceremonies are of ancient date and splendor. The time-hallowed cherry dance was led by a twinkle-toed ballerina, whose age was ninety-nine— a dancer of the greatest renown, Haruko Katayama. She had tripped the cherry dance for nearly seventy years, and had lived through the reigns of five emperors. The report was that she danced like a damsel of twenty, as nimbly and gracefully as the girls she led —three hundred and sixty of them. As the first ballerina, she inspected the noses, necks and eyelids of the girls. Noses and necks must be as white as the moon, eyelids must be as delicately pink as the rose. Then Haruko Katayama, in her ninety-ninth year, led her three hundred and sixty girls in the cherry dance.

Musicians played ancient Shinto melodies, while the priests waved laurel branches at the four points of the compass, driving away evil forces. Then wine was brought in thimble cups, and the bride and bridegroom each drank nine cups of wine. Thereupon the wedding was complete, the marriage alliance between Japan and puppet Manchukuo.

For the first time an American woman penetrated the heart of the Arabian peninsula. Two of them—a Mrs. Dame and a Mrs. Van Peursem, in the company of Mrs. Dame's husband, an American doctor. I learned of this from Dr. F. M. Potter of the Board of Foreign Missions of the Reformed Church. These American women, dressed like Arabs, went veiled to the court of Ibn Saud in the little-known city of Riadh.

The ladies were placed in quarters where there happened to be no bathroom. When Ibn Saud heard of this he commanded that the adjoining apartment be turned into a bathroom. This adjoining apartment was occupied by the Sheik of Public Order and his harem. The carpenters got the royal orders at midnight, and immediately evicted the sheik and his harem. The American ladies were awakened by workmen knocking down the wall of their room. In Arabia, when the King spoke, the order must be carried out on the instant.

Ibn Saud employed an American engineer, and one morning he commanded the American to come at once. That meant not a moment's delay. The engineer was having his morning tub. So he was taken down the street clad only in a bath towel. When he got to the palace he found the King wanted to introduce him to a lady. That was all.

Mrs. Dame said that Ibn Saud's boast was that he had had one hundred and fifty-three wives, and had divorced one hundred and fifty. And of the divorced spouses, not one had gone away angry at him. One wife was the mother of thirteen children and had been married to the King twice. He wedded her and then divorced her. Whereupon one of his brothers married her. The King decided he wanted her back, so he made his brother divorce her, and wedded her again. That bit of royal conduct was okay. In fact, the King's taking the lady from her second husband, his brother, made all according to Hoyle—or rather according to the Koran. It's a Moslem law that if a man divorces a wife he cannot remarry her until she has been married and divorced by someone else. Well, *Allah hu el akbar*.

No gay and frivolous philanderer was the husband of a hundred and fifty-odd wives. He was a Puritan, a stern, severe moralist, the leader of the Wahibi, the killjoys of the central Arabian desert. Ibn Saud and his Wahibis were opposed to almost every kind of fun and amusement—except marriage.

Marry early and often, commanded Mohammed the Prophet, and the fierce warrior Ibn Saud obeyed like a good Moslem. The Koran allowed four wives. He had only three at a time, because he liked to keep one place open at all times for a new wife.

Ibn Saud, the dour Puritan, didn't marry for mere entertainment. When he made a treaty with another tribe, he took a wife from that tribe as a kind of signature to the treaty. He was a great diplomat and made many treaties. In fact, he liked to make treaties.

Marriage to Ibn Saud meant even more than that. Once he was wounded in battle, wounded so badly that his tribesmen believed he was as good as dead. They were about to desert him, and select a more able-bodied chief. But Ibn Saud shouted a loud command: "Get me another wife. I feel like getting married again." He immediately celebrated another wedding. So his tribesmen figured the old boy was just about as good as new.

Yet it was related that Ibn Saud, of so many wives, really loved only one woman. She was the Princess Jauhara. He married her when he was a young man and made her his queen. But not long after she died. The fierce Ibn Saud was broken-hearted and remained broken-hearted thereafter. He got married over and over again out of sorrow.

The apex of his power, increased so greatly by matrimonial politics, came when he assailed and conquered an ancient kingdom. Word of this came with the news of the death of the Iman of the Kingdom of Coffee. Certainly the honor of being called the coffee monarchy was to be given to the fabulous land of Yemen, with its famous city of Mocha. That name stood as the symbol and pride of the fragrant brown bean that gives us our morning libation.

Zaidi Iman Yahya, the Lord of Yemen, passed to the bosom of Allah not at the height of his fortune but at the depth of his misfortune. Better to be among the houris of Paradise than in his own fair kingdom of coffee—for Ibn Saud, the fanatical, was raging with the terror of war.

Few corners of the earth are more legendary and fascinating than that southwest section of the great Arabian peninsula—the Yemen, where the desert blooms like a rose, the land of that mysterious conquering race of ancient times, the Sabean. Its king, its Iman, reigned for many a year as a great potentate of that remote region. But out in the desert of the camel-riding tribes was Ibn Saud, ruler of the Wahibis. Ibn Saud built an empire of the desert and threatened to seize everything in Arabia.

It was the hard luck of the Iman of Yemen, just as it had been the luckless chance of King Hussein of Mecca, to get into difficulties with Ibn Saud. They had a dispute over a minor stretch of desert called the Land of Yam—it seemed as if the fierce Lord of the Wahabis were out to make all Arabia his yam.

There was a conflict of arms and, strangely enough,

such modernities as airplanes, tanks and the radio played their part in that war of the primitive desert. Ibn Saud had them. Ibn Saud, the Puritan, had gone modern. The fighting men of Yemen were beaten and disorganized, and the land of coffee became the spoil of the enemy. So the Iman of Yemen may well have felt that this climax of disaster was a good time to pass along to the gardens and fountains of Paradise where the gazelle-eyed maidens smile upon the faithful.

While war clouds surrounded the King of Kings at Addis Ababa, legal difficulties surrounded the nephew of the King of Kings in the south of France. It was a love story, with the passionate suitor biting off the lady's nose. The passionate suitor in question bore the same name as his uncle, the conquering Lion of Judah. He was called Araya Hailie Selassie. At Chambery, in the languorous land of Languedoc, he was sentenced to a year in jail, which sentence he appealed. His defense was that it was the burning power of volcanic African love that caused him to bite off the lady's nose. Anyway, he merely snipped off the tip, and she had it grafted back into place, so that her nose was as good as new.

It was an unhappy ending to the story of how the nephew of the Emperor of Ethiopia, sojourning in Europe, fell in love with Yamile, daughter of an Egyptian newspaper editor. He loved her, but she didn't love him. He proposed marriage, but she wasn't marrying. He tried to persuade her to elope, but she wasn't eloping. He bombarded her with letters and telegrams, but she wasn't surrendering. Finally, he sent a friend to her, who told her how the melancholy lover was desperately ill, calling for her, and that he would surely die unless she went to see him.

So the lovely Yamile hurried to his supposed bedside, found him hale and hearty—merely eager to renew his sentimental expostulations. She kept on saying "No" until he made one last plea—that he might kiss her good-bye forever. She said—if it was really good-bye and also forever, okay. But instead of kissing her he bit off her nose.

It must have been something like this: "I love your eyes, your hair, your lips—I love your nose."

"Ouch!"

A young man went into a five-and-ten-cent store. He was waited on by a singularly attractive and courteous girl. The young man left his purse behind, whether by accident or design, the record did not say. The clerk, a pretty damsel named Viola Brown, kept it for him. When he returned, she greeted him with a smile and "Hello, here's your purse." Said the young man: "One good turn deserves another. After holding my purse for me, the least you can do is come to dinner."

"Well," said the young lady, "if you put it that way——"

That dinner was followed by others. The young man

in question turned out to be James K. Lin, adopted
son of no less a potentate than the President of China.
He was over here as an undergraduate at Ohio State
University. The sequel to the story was that wedding
bells would chime. They would, that is, provided His
Excellency the President of China consented. For
young Mr. James K. Lin was a dutiful follower of
Confucius, and respected the wishes of his parents.

The sequel thereupon had a sequel—not so rosy and
romantic. In the first place Miss Viola Brown, the
five-and-ten salesgirl, denied that she was engaged to
James Lin, the adopted son of the Chinese President.
She stated they were already married. Secondly, James
Lin said there must be some mistake. He claimed they
were not married. He averred that they got no further
toward the matrimonial altar than a cable which he
sent to his adopted father asking for permission to
marry the young lady. Thirdly, he got an answer to
that cable, and the answer was "No"—permission refused.

So if they were engaged, they were forbidden to
marry—while if they were already married, that was
forbidden also.

Grave matters of statecraft were en-
livened by a demand made upon the government at
London by an Oriental sultana. She put in a claim
that the British were in possession of islands that didn't
belong to them, and should turn them over to her own
realm. This exotic potentate was a former co-ed of the

University of Illinois. Illinois '27, Princess Tarhata Kiran.

She was a niece of that monarch with a musical comedy title—the Sultan of Sulu. Her education, so very American, had been an academic success. She had been the pride of the campus at the University of Illinois, excellent at studies, a leader in social activities. In every respect the princess from the islands of Sulu had made her mark in class affairs at the Midwestern college, and had become a member of a national sorority.

After graduating from college she went back to her native land, the Mohammedan monarchy of Sulu in the southern Philippine Islands. There she fell in love, and that caused a startling transformation in the Illinois co-ed. She married a Moro chief, became his fifth wife. She let her bobbed hair grow long and gave up the short dresses of college days, had her teeth filed in native fashion, and took up an Oriental existence in the harem of a warrior lord of the Moros.

Her husband was a veteran fighting man. He had battled against Uncle Sam away back in the days of the Philippine Insurrection, and not long after his marriage to the graduate of the University of Illinois he went on the warpath again. He headed a revolt against the American authorities at Manila. The former college girl joined her husband in the rebellion. She took a large part in the disturbances that finally resulted in the capture of the Moro chief. He was sentenced to a prison term.

Soon afterward she was adopted by her uncle, the

Sultan of Sulu, as his daughter. Presently the Sultan was appointed a Senator and sat in the Philippine legislature, representing the Mohammedans of his kingdom. During his absence the former Illinois college girl acted as absolute monarch, and in that capacity made a demand through diplomatic channels, asking Great Britain to give up a couple of islands south of the Philippines—islands which long have been claimed to be a part of the Kingdom of Sulu.

P.S. She didn't get the islands.

The Moros, those fierce Mohammedan islanders, might not seem to be the sort to have had trouble because of the ambitious women who aspired to rule. Yet such was the case. For example, much disturbance followed the death of the aged Sultan, His Highness Padukka Mahasari Mana Manaluna Hadji Mohammed Jamalul Kiram II. He left no sons, only a daughter, the Princess Dayang-Dayang. She thought she'd make herself the ruling sultana.

A powerful party, headed by the Grand Vizier, opposed. Such mighty warriors as the Sulus, they vowed, would never be ruled by a woman. After a bitter controversy, they dispossessed the Princess Dayang-Dayang and gave the crown to the old Sultan's brother, Rajah Muda Mawalil Wasit Kiram.

The Princess Dayang-Dayang seemed to resign herself to the loss of the crown. She visited the new sultan with humility and submission. Shortly thereafter the

167

monarch fell ill, and he was dying. The official version is that he succumbed to a heart attack, but the rumor spread—poison.

Still the Princess Dayang-Dayang did not get the throne. The party against her vowed once more that the Moros of Sulu would not be ruled by a sultana. So they crowned a new sultan of Sulu, His Majesty Fainal Abireen II. This convinced the Princess Dayang-Dayang that the Moros would never bend to the beardless femininity of a sultana. So what did she do?

She utilized the institution with which ambitious women have often masked their power—matrimony. Princess Dayang-Dayang possessed a husband, and had him crowned sultan. Muskets and firecrackers crashed in salute as nine Imans placed the Sulu diadem on the head of His Highness Ombra Amilbangsa, who went on the warpath to compel his claim. So the Moros of Sulu, instead of being governed by a sultana, were ruled by two sultans embattled against each other—and the power behind one of the thrones was Princess Dayang-Dayang.

In Paris the Chamber of Deputies voted to double a woman's pension—though it was unusual for the supreme law-making body of France to take time out for special action on one single person. But then the woman was an ex-queen, former monarch of a romantic realm. The story went afar to some remote bits of tropical land that might perhaps be called the Islands of Vanilla.

The Comoro Islands are in the Mozambique Channel between Madagascar and the African mainland—down Zanzibar way. They are rich bits of land which produce many things—especially vanilla, the bean that produces the fragrant flavoring for our cakes. One of the islands is called Moheli, and years ago the Lordship of Moheli fell by inheritance to a girl princess.

She was a comely young queen, quite brown and tropical, as the people of the islands were. It was thought best that as a full-fledged monarch she should learn something of the ways of European civilization. The French were predominant in those parts, and she went for a bit of schooling to the Island of Réunion, east of French Madagascar.

She was received with royal honors there—a file of French soldiers drawn up at salute. The soldiers were Zouaves. They wore the sprightly Zouave uniform so familiar in those days—the snappy cap and the baggy red trousers. The young queen from the Islands of Vanilla gazed in admiration. She thought she had never seen such fetching warriors before—one in particular, a dashing young Zouave whose trousers seemed redder and baggier than any others and who curled his mustaches in the smartest Parisian fashion. The girl queen fell in love then and there. She felt she couldn't live without that Zouave. He, on his part, was not unmindful of the dignity of a queen, even though a trifle dusky. So they were married.

It might be supposed that the young couple then

ruled as King and Queen of Vanilla, but not at all. The Zouave didn't want to give up his military post and his prospects of promotion for a dubious barbaric kingdom. So she donated her island realm to the French Republic, and the Queen of Vanilla became mere Madame Camille Paul. In return the Government of Paris gave her a pension of two hundred dollars a year. Later the pension was raised to three hundred dollars a year. Then in time the red-trousered Zouave took his queen wife back to France, and there they lived for years—quite comfortably.

But it was the old story—the depression. An investment or two went to the bad, and presently the former Queen of the Islands of Vanilla, now an old woman, had nothing left except that government pension. But she could hardly live on three hundred dollars a year. She appealed to the Government in Paris. The Chamber of Deputies itself took action, and doubled the pension of the dusky queen who gave up a vanilla throne to become Madame Zouave.

X

Famous Beauties

In this category we find the woman who gets her man; the charming one plagued by unwelcome wooing; the creature of excessive loveliness whose fascinations are ruinous, fatal beauty; and the enchantress of bygone times who has outlived her grace and fortune and has only memories. The tales of these vary from broad comedy to infinite pathos.

❦

Peggy Upton Archer Hopkins Joyce Morner got married again. The Countess Gosta Morner, more celebrated in the lists of love as Peggy Joyce, took her fifth. In making this known, a New York make-up editor permitted himself an unconscious flight of humor. In one column he ran the story relating that Peggy was to take husband number five. In the adjoining column he had a headline reading: "The Moon Will Wear a Veil."

Peggy was no mere fledgling. According to the most learned genealogists she was now well over forty. The blushing bridegroom, Dr. Vivian Jackson, was a thirty-year-old professor of astro-physics at the University of London.

Our Peggy was only seventeen when she ran away from school to marry a young man from Denver. That one lasted six months. Mr. Peggy Number Two was Sherburne Hopkins of Washington, D. C. By this time the lady had learned it was just as easy to fall in love with a rich man as a poor one, and a darn sight more comfortable. After two years Peggy was in circulation again, but not for long. Number Three was J. Stanley Joyce, a Midwestern lumber millionaire. Married in 1920; divorced in 1921.

Her third marriage left her in such comfortable circumstances that three years later she was able to afford herself the luxury of a Swedish count. Number Four was Count Morner. That one endured four years—four long years, but its reaction upon Peggy was summed up in the vow, "Never again," which she publicly uttered in 1928. She changed her mind. The romance of the ex-countess and Professor Jackson was born through a common love for horses. In addition to his distinction in the realm of astro-physics, Dr. Jackson was an accomplished steeplechase rider.

A day or two previously the cables from London brought the news that Peggy had been having an argument with the management of the hotel where she lived. She was annoyed to find sand in her bed when she went to retire. According to the next London dispatch, it was not sand, it was another husband.

Nimble-legged Marilyn Miller was seeing a friend off on the *Bremen*. She and several others in the party did not heed the "All ashore that's going ashore" signal. So they, without so much as a toothbrush or a passport to help them on their journey, were carried all the way to Europe. Among those in the party was Don Alvarado, the movie actor.

When the *Bremen* arrived at Cherbourg, Miss Miller wanted to go to Paris to see her ex-husband, Jack Pickford, who was ill there. But the French authorities said nay, because the graceful Miller was not equipped with a passport.

She went on to Southampton, where John Bull's authorities said Miss Miller and Mr. Alvarado could stay in London until a boat was on its way back to America. While there, Marilyn announced her engagement to marry Don Alvarado. The unintended voyage had produced the results so often accomplished by the moon and the sea.

Arthur Casper of San Bernadino, California, was a Lily Pons fan. He wrote several letters to La Pons at her Norwalk, Connecticut, home, but got no reply. That did not deter him—it seems to have encouraged him. He packed his bags, and traveled all the way across the continent. From New York he took a taxi to Norwalk, Connecticut, which cost him twelve dollars. At Norwalk he went to the home where the soprano lived with her husband. He buzzed at the front door, and got no reply. He went to a side door, which he found open, and walked right in, a suitcase in each hand—moving in.

Lily Pons was not at home, but her mother was—and she was indeed astonished when she looked down the stairs and saw Casper with his two suitcases. "What are you doing here?" cried Mama.

"I am looking for Lily," Casper replied. "I am one of her public. I'll follow her to the end of the earth to talk to her."

Mama had her wits about her and she told Casper to go to the kitchen and she'd get some coffee for him, and at the same time whispered to a servant to call the police.

So Casper the fan had coffee with the mother of his idol. He told her some more about how he'd follow Lily to the end of the earth, to which Mama responded with a proper admonition—didn't he know that Lily was married and had a husband?

"What difference does that make between friends?" Casper replied grandly.

Just then the cops walked in, at which Casper exclaimed in soulful disillusion: "I came all the way from California to see Lily, and the police pounce in on me!"

The police not only pounced in, but held Casper on charge of trespass, which was calculated to teach him that the proper procedure for an ardent Lily Pons fan was to buy tickets for the Metropolitan Opera—at seven dollars apiece.

Some days later a Pons admirer was found in the lady's geranium bed. The Pons gardener made the discovery. When asked what he was doing among the flowers, the intruder replied that he was a detective, Sleuth X-3, sent to Norwalk by the Philadelphia court authorities. The police demanded his credentials. Whereupon he produced a detective's diploma from a mail order firm, a suitcase, an umbrella, a typewriter, some detective magazines, the plots of two plays, and a batch of sheet music. "What do you mean you were sent by the Philadelphia court authorities?" inquired the cops.

Detective X-3 produced a letter from Judge Curtiss Bach of Philadelphia. He explained that he had written to Judge Bach, outlining a plan to protect Miss Pons from annoyers. The judge had replied, advising X-3 to mind his own business. "But one of the words in the letter was blurred," said X-3, "and I thought he meant, go ahead."

Arraigned in the Norwalk police court, the prosecutor told him he would be charged with "constigation."

"Do you know what that means?" the prosecutor demanded sternly.

"Sure," said Detective X-3, "certainly I know."

"Well," said the prosecutor, "you're a better man than I am, because I don't."

Detective X-3 was sentenced to three months in jail, but the judge suspended sentence upon the prisoner's promise to go home with his detective badge, his typewriter, his umbrella, his suitcase, his detective magazines, his plays, his sheet music and everything. The Norwalk authorities thereupon turned him over to a rabbi, who undertook to determine whether X-3 was harmless or not.

Simultaneous complications relating to matrimony and blackmail befell Mae West—queen of plumpness and pulchritude. In the matrimonial mix-up, it was not that Mae was thinking about entering into wedlock. She was trying to prove that she was entirely outside of that holy estate. A vaudeville actor insisted that he was her husband, claiming that he had married the buxom blonde back in 1911, when she was presumably not so buxom, but undoubtedly just as blond. He went to court trying to prove it.

The wedded or unwedded star started legal proceedings of her own. She called upon the law to protect her against those matrimonial claims. She vowed she didn't know the man, had never seen him; didn't want to know him, didn't want to see him. He might be somebody's husband, but not hers.

While thus haunted by allegations of marriage, Mae West was further bedeviled by threats of blackmail—

wicked plots and diabolical conspiracies weaving around those ample charms. The plots and conspiracies were crooked. The charms were curved. Delicate nostrils might have scented the trail of the press agent. But the story was no wisp of illusion, any more than Mae herself was a wisp of illusion. The Los Angeles police made a wholesale catch of prisoners, five men in all. Five were plenty, even for a Mae West picture. Four, however, were released. Only one remained in jail, vowing that he was innocent.

It all caused Mae a good deal of distress. Her blond tresses in disarray—as when a heroine weeps in distress. She received five menacing letters demanding money. The blackmailer threatened to take her life or spoil her beauty. Maybe he meant take her beauty and spoil her life. Directions were given for placing the money. Los Angeles detectives set a series of traps, one after each demand for money. Four times—nothing doing. The blackmailer wrote back that conditions had not been just right.

In his fifth letter he directed that Mae should answer by printing her telephone number in a newspaper want ad. That was the limit. Mae was terrified. She told reporters: "I guess the note that ordered me to put my telephone number in the papers scared me the most. I'd have had a lot of strange people calling me." Coming up to see her, sometime. The police set another trap, placed the money, and the detectives laid in ambush.

This was in a prominent Hollywood hotel, the package of money deposited in the front of a palm. A man came along, looked cautiously around and reached for the money. The detectives reached for him. They also reached for four other men who were near by. The prisoner who did the grabbing turned out to be a bus boy in a Hollywood studio restaurant. The four others proved to the satisfaction of the police that they were merely sauntering around the palm-lined haunt in Hollywood. They were released. The bus boy was charged with extortion. He explained that he saw a man place a package in the front of the palm and wondered what it was, so he thought he'd look and see. He looked and saw too much. The cops didn't believe the explanation.

That having been that, the Mae West matrimonial tangle went dragging through the courts, with the star of the ample charms finally admitting that she had been married to the one-time song and dance man. Then the final hearing came up at Hollywood, the "forgotten husband" suing for one thousand dollars a month.

"For over thirty years I've kept this secret in my heart," he said plaintively. And he thought that all those years of silence deserved a reward—Mae West to support him at the expense of one thousand dollars a month.

The lady with curves, on her part, sued the "forgotten husband" for divorce—charging that he had deserted her after they had been married a month and later on had married another woman.

The case came to a surprise conclusion. The forgotten husband announced that an agreement had been made. His lawyer called it "a nominal settlement."

Rumor said the settlement involved the payment of a few hundred dollars, and Mae got her divorce. So that's how it ended—he was forgotten for thirty years, then made himself remembered. Now, presumably, he could go on being forgotten again.

❦

Some years ago Lya De Putti, the film actress, died in New York and then came word that her husband had committed suicide over in their native land of Hungary. That brought to light a strange turn of drama. For twelve years, while the brilliant star of the screen was making a career for herself, she was regarded as dead by her husband and two daughters in Budapest. Her husband pretended that she had died, and her two children believed it. It was only after her actual death that the two girls learned that the fascinating beauty of the screen, Lya De Putti, was their mother.

She had married Zoltan von Szepessy, a proud Hungarian aristocrat who was an official of the Austro-Hungarian imperial court. For a while they were happy, but in 1920 the radiant young wife left her husband and went on the stage. This was a dreadful blow to the haughty aristocrat. He never became reconciled to it. From then on he considered his wife dead. He spoke of her as one no longer in the land of the living. He had a grave arranged in a cemetery, an empty grave above which was a headstone bearing the name of his wife and giving the day she left him as the date of her death. Thus he lived a life of tragical make-believe.

Meanwhile, the beautiful wife, using her maiden name, made her sensational success on the motion-picture screen. Yet the husband never gave up the hope that she would return, renounce the theatrical career that he hated, and return to her family. But she never did return. Instead she died, and he killed himself. He left a note with the command that he should be buried beside that empty grave in the Budapest cemetery, the empty tomb that he had arranged when he began to live the fiction that his wife was dead.

More than half a century ago a sprightly and most attractive young American actress went to London. In a long-forgotten musical show called "Little Christopher Columbus" she became the hit of the town. She not only delighted the gallery crowds, but also found favor with London society, which took her up with enthusiasm.

Her name, May Yohe. She was once the owner of the famous Hope diamond. She was married to the son of a duke, Lord Francis Hope. Thus the famous Hope diamond passed for a while into her hands. It was supposed to be a brilliant marriage. Then there was a nine-day sensation when it became known that May Yohe had left the Duke's son, social position, Hope diamond and everything for the love of a dashing American adventurer—Captain Putnam Bradlee Strong, son of the mayor of Boston.

That began a cycle of unhappy years. From time to time people would hear of a once handsome woman singing in small playhouses, a woman bearing a strong resemblance to the once gorgeous and glittering May Yohe. They even heard of her selling tickets in movie theaters.

The last heard of her was in a W.P.A. story. The famous May Yohe applied for a W.P.A. job, but found she could not get one because she had lost her citizenship. She took an oath as an American citizen in a federal court in Boston, and thus qualified for federal relief. May Yohe, once the darling of Mayfair and Belgravia, a seventy-two-year-old W.P.A. worker!

Here's a tale of long years and changeless sentiment. In Chicago a woman of seventy-two was on relief. Yet in the time of her distant youth she had been a beauty of the theater—the toast of Broadway, as they used to say, a member of the Floradora Sextette. Back in those dimly remembered days she married Willis Reeves. That was in 1887. A few years later they were divorced—more than half a century ago—when the Floradora girl was a queen of toasts at Rector's and Delmonico's.

The passing of years—the passing of youth, beauty, fame and money. Mrs. Margaret Reeves, seventy-two—and on relief. But she didn't stay on it. Willis Reeves

died. His will was made public. He left all his posses-
sions to his one-time wife, a tidy sum of many thousands of dollars.

When she heard it, the old woman sighed and said:
"Willis must have loved me better than I knew—perhaps too much." A little late to realize that. Anyway,
Willis never forgot his Floradora girl of fifty years before.

❧

Here is a tale bleak and bitter. Yet it
glints with a streak of pride luminous yet tragic—this
tale of faded youth.

Famous among the lovely ones of the earth, Sylvia
Gough. Some may remember her, the toast of fashionable London and the stage. Her father was a fabulous
financier of South Africa gold, associated with Cecil
Rhodes. A girl dowered with millions, she was presented at St. James's Court as a debutante, and then
and there flashed to fame as one of the world's most
beautiful women.

She glittered on with a social career of brilliance and
adoration. The eminent painter, Augustus John, im-
mortalized her in one of the finest of his master works,
"The Portrait of Sylvia Gough." She took her fair face
and figure onto the stage, to gleam before the foot-
lights. She appeared as a star beauty in the musical
comedy, "The Right Girl," in New York.

Life and luck for Sylvia Gough went on the down-
grade. She was stricken by the coming of years, the go-

ing of her fortune. The depth was seen in London at a murder trial in which she appeared as a witness. She was faded, haggard, beaten by life. She had been earning a meager living by working at odd jobs as a model, a model for drab and pitiful character parts, not for her one-time soul-stirring beauty.

On the witness stand she told the story of a killing, a story dark, drab, pitiful. A Bohemian party in London. Two men quarreled and fought. A blow with a studio hammer, one killed. Both men young, brilliant, one a well-known London book reviewer of thirty, the other a promising author of twenty. And this was the flash of pride, the luminous and the tragic. They fought because of her. One abused her in a lover's quarrel, the other sprang to her defense and struck the deadly blow. Men still fighting over Sylvia Gough, who once was so lovely.

There's an ever-recurring theme in the affairs of mankind—the great who have fallen low, someone who has walked the dizzy heights of fame and splendor, then dies in obscurity, in a garret, poor and alone. That was the story of Dolores, she who had been the dazzling Queen of Beauty, the toast of London, worshiped and acclaimed.

Who was Dolores? She always said that her mother was the daughter of Count Fournier, a general in the French Army. Her father was an obscure English actor. When the aristocratic French girl married the actor, she was cast off by her family, the élite of the French nobility. So Dolores was born and grew up in the Bloomsbury district of London.

She became a dancer and swiftly climbed to fame because of the exotic allure of her art and her singular and flawless beauty. Soon she was the favorite model of Epstein, that renowned and bizarre genius of sculpture. He glorified her extravagantly. She was supreme as London's great beauty, a crowned queen among the artists and writers of London's Bohemia. In 1920, Ziegfeld brought her to America to preside as a world-famous beauty in the Ziegfeld Follies.

An exotic legend grew up around her. Dolores believed that her beauty was not a mere thing of a day, but had come down through the ages, by reincarnation. In her pride she once wrote: "My beauty is a survival from the undying past. Was I Venus," she asked, "or did I, who have never yet found the ideal love, only embody the torturous desires and rapturous fulfillment of passion?"

A young artist of great promise, Frederick Atkinson, fell in love with her. He showered her with jewels and luxuries, spent his fortune on her. Then he killed himself, leaving behind a note of strange, poetic adoration. This is what he wrote:

> "O child of pain,
> Dolores!
> Thy fatal star doth beckon on to doom;
> Seek not thou for happiness,
> For in the book of time,

Stained with the tears of blood and martyred souls,
Is set a seal;
And on it fixed thy name
Dolores."

After the tragic suicide of the young artist, Dolores disappeared from public view. Perhaps she had come to the conclusion that she was only "the embodiment of torturous desires." Aristocratic London saw her no more on the stage, no more in the dance.

Some years later came the news of her death at forty, penniless, obscure. She had been making her living in a cheap amusement center, exhibited as the "Fasting Woman." She had been on display sitting in a barrel, haggard and emaciated, wasted by illness—ballyhooed as the woman who lived without food, fasting.

So ended Dolores, once London's greatest beauty of whom the tragic young artist with a despairing hand had written: "O child of pain, Dolores!"

Nobody who grew up in the Western mining country at the turn of the century could fail to have had impressed on his mind the silver-dollar fame and splendor of H. A. W. Tabor. As I myself was reared in the mining camp of Cripple Creek, the name Tabor is like a glamorous symbol dominating early memory. He was the top-notch and overshadowing example of a money-coining, money-tossing, gold-and-silver-flaunting king of the bonanza era. His wife,

Baby Doe, was a queen to match her king, with her beauty, her laughter and the stunning brilliance of her personality. When they were married, the President of the United States, Chester A. Arthur, attended the wedding.

The apogee of their splendor was in Washington, where Silver King Tabor strutted in the dignity of a United States Senator. He went by appointment for thirty days as the Senator from Colorado, and legends flared of the spendthrift munificence of the Silver Senator and his wife, Baby Doe. They say he wore a nightshirt studded with diamonds.

Yet I have heard it said by old-timers in the West that Tabor, King of Silver, started the breaks going against him when he made that glamorous marriage—when he ditched his Old Woman. She had stuck along with him through many a hard year when he was little more than a roustabout and a hanger-on at the mining camps. In those poverty days he ran across two shoemakers who had abandoned half-soles and uppers and gone mine hunting in Colorado. Tabor grubstaked the pair and they struck a fabulously rich vein of silver in Leadville. It made them all wealthy, and Tabor went on to acquire further mines, which made him the Silver Croesus of the West. In Denver, he built the spectacular million-dollar Tabor Opera House—a phenomenon of grandeur in the West. And all the time he had the Old Woman with him.

Then, at the height of his wealth, he met Elizabeth McCourt Doe, whom they called Baby Doe. Young and flashingly beautiful! As Tabor had the Old Woman, so

Baby Doe had a husband. But these impediments didn't count in the face of the immense power of the Silver King. And the old-timers say that when Tabor discarded the Old Woman to marry Baby Doe, he busted his string of luck. Certain it is that not long after the riotously splendid wedding and the brief senatorial career in Washington, things took a swift turn for the worse.

The gold standard was put into effect. Silver was no longer the metallic base of American currency. All of Tabor's wealth was in silver. The financial rocks were before him, and his fortune declined swiftly. He sank to poverty and died. Years later one of his daughters, whom he had christened Silver Dollar Tabor, died in a cheap rooming house in Chicago. Miss Silver Dollar Tabor had tried to become an author, but she had tried in vain.

Tabor always told his wife Baby Doe to hang on to the Matchless Mine. It had been the chief source of his wealth. It had petered out, but he always believed it would come back. And Baby Doe believed it too. She clung to the mine with a pathetic fidelity, so much so that she became a Western legend. She lived in a shack near the shaft of the Matchless Mine and worked in rough overalls and a man's shirt, digging and prospecting.

It was there that she was found, frozen to death in the mine shack—seventy-three years old. No, she wasn't dressed in rough overalls and a man's shirt when they found her. She was wearing faded, feminine finery, the remnants of a wardrobe that had once been made for her by fashionable dressmakers. She had put her old-time glory on before she lay down to freeze. She had two wrinkled bills, the last two dollars of the fabulous fortune of the Silver King.

They were getting ready to tear down an old New York hotel, and moved out an ancient recluse. She was Mrs. Ida Wood, age ninety-three years. They found three-quarters of a million dollars in her room. They discovered money, money, money—money hidden everywhere. From a secret pocket that she had sewed in her dress they took fifty ten-thousand-dollar bills—half a million dollars in all!

She lived in that same hotel room for fourteen years. She seldom went out. She cooked her own meals in the room, sending a bell boy to the store for a few cents' worth of provisions at a time. And all the while she had that money with her, hidden away in strange places. Thousand-dollar bills buried in heaps of rubbish, five-thousand-dollar bills under the bathtub. So much of it that some of this hidden treasure she had forgotten.

Years ago the old recluse was a reigning beauty of New York. Her husband was Benjamin Wood, a power in the city, the owner and editor of one of the most important newspapers of the time, the old New York *Daily News*. He was a great sporting character, Editor Wood, a mighty gambler of those gaudy years in the nineties. They tell how one night he won a hundred thousand dollars in a gambling house. When he went home he counted it out in front of his wife and gave her fifty thousand. It was all according to arrangement. She allowed him to gamble as much as he pleased, so long as he gave her half of his winnings.

At Saratoga on one occasion he broke the bank in a glittering gambling house. He took away a hundred and fifty thousand dollars, and split it half and half with his wife. When Editor Wood died, his widow sold his paper, the old New York *Daily News*. A large part of the purchase price she received in thousand-dollar bills. This was typical finance with the radiant woman who was one of the beauties of New York. It was money, always money. She got it and kept it. As for banks—no, not at all. She kept it in cash.

The years went by. Editor Wood and his former newspaper and his once beautiful wife—they were almost forgotten. Ida Wood grew old. She lived with her money, fondled her collection of banknotes. She became a recluse, living in her hotel room and thinking up odd ways to hide her wealth. No, they said she wasn't mad. She was as clear- and sound-minded as any old lady you'll find. She merely had an eccentricity. She loved to have her money near her and hide it away, in ten-thousand-dollar bills. Only the tearing down of the hotel disclosed her secret—with a treasure hunt in the belongings of the one-time belle of New York.

Boston had a feminine mash mystery. A woman kiss-and-run terrorist deeply scandalized the city of the Puritans. It used to be a crime in Boston for a man to kiss his wife in public, but now it was a case of men being forcibly kissed, not by their wives, but by a ruthless, seductive Amazon. She seized a shrinking male in her powerful arms, imprinted a kiss of brutal violence on his chaste and modest lips, and then fled.

The first word of the kissing woman prowler came when a big, burly Bostonian rushed into a police station and shouted: "Can't a decent man go about the streets without being attacked by a ruffian woman?" He told how he was walking along, sedate and demure, when a woman rushed up to him, seized him, pinned his arms to his sides, and kissed him repeatedly. Then, before he could call for help, she had darted away—curse her!

No wonder the men of Boston were terrified. The honor of manhood was threatened by a wild woman. So the men were calling upon stalwart American womanhood, pleading: "Think of your brothers, your sons, your husbands, and protect them!"

XI

Lady Killers

The lady killer, as well as the queen of
hearts, has a place in any pageant of romance. Yet I find that
my story collection does not present the great lover as frequently or as devotionally as it does his sister in fascination.
This accords with history and legend. There is the supreme
Don Juan and there is the lesser Casanova, but the record
celebrates many more devastating ladies than male charmers.

History is poor, I think, in examples of great lovers romanc-
ing with fatal beauties. How magnificent it would be to have
Don Juan mated with Cleopatra, Casanova with Peggy Joyce!
In my own album of the soul's infatuation, I find no such
miracles.

The New York theater and night club set was buzzing with gossip. Who would prevail in the affections of John Barrymore—daughter or ex-wife?

The magnificent, though aging, Barrymore made a much heralded return to Broadway—a return after seventeen years. He opened in "My Dear Children." All sorts of Barrymore eccentricities had been expected at the performance. There was one eccentricity, but not Barrymore's. While John was making a speech between the acts, some guy dressed as Hamlet leaped on the stage.

"I'm Hamlet's ghost," he cried, and tried to embrace Barrymore.

But the great Barrymore did not fancy the embraces of ghosts.

At the end of the performance one person who failed to get into the Barrymore dressing room to offer congratulations was his former wife, Elaine Barrie. She was the heroine of the romance when he was Caliban and she was Ariel. Elaine was kept out of the dressing room by John's daughter, Diana Barrymore Blythe—progeny of Barrymore and the society poetess of yesteryear, Michael Strange. The ex-wife, the former Ariel, in no wise daunted, went to the night club where she knew the Barrymores had a table arranged. There the proud daughter sat beside her equally proud father; but alas, the proud daughter got up to dance, and while she was away from the table, the equally proud ex-wife slid into her place. And when she returned, there were John and Elaine in a tête-à-tête. Whereupon the not-so-proud daughter went home.

After that eventful reunion with his estranged wife, Barrymore seemed likely to make it not only a marital reunion but also a stage reunion. For a time Elaine Barrie had played with him in the comedy he now had brought to Broadway. Then her place had been taken by a blond actress, Doris Dudley. She was regarded as a Barrymore protégée and, moreover, was a bosom friend of Barrymore's daughter Diana, who was so angrily hostile toward wife Elaine.

Broadway reports were that Elaine would go back into the play, and Doris would lose her job. To which Doris responded with the following philosophical and cynical expression: "I'm in the peculiar position of trying to fight sex with talent." The answer would seem to be, talent hasn't a chance in that kind of contest.

The question seemed to be, who would get spanked. In the play "My Dear Children," actor Barrymore spanked one of his dear children—the one played successively by wife Elaine and protégée Doris. Rumor said that matrimonial trouble had ensued when one night on the stage John spanked Elaine too hard. Possibly there had been some sort of domestic misunderstanding, something of the sort that often makes a husband want to spank his wife, spank her good and plenty. Anyway, the magnificent Barrymore is said to have laid his hand on Elaine with much more vigor than the drama called for. She was furious, left hubby, and quit the play.

The Barrymore reconciliation had legal aspects too —for Elaine had a divorce suit pending out West. The two had made exciting legal history. First Elaine divorced John, then she canceled it. John entered a separation suit against Elaine, and then dropped it. Whereupon she started another divorce suit. That one was pending. Moreover, John sued Elaine and her mother for an accounting of three hundred thousand dollars of his money. That also was pending. Things always seemed to be pending with the Barrymores—trouble, for example.

The love life of the great Barrymore had been publicized so much that it was getting to be rather stale—and what could be worse than a love life grown stale? But consider the dilemma the Great Profile faced. Of course, a profile should be able to face things, but the features of the headlined Barrymore predicament were really intricate.

The reconciliation of John and Elaine did not work out, and new battles ensued. John became so annoyed with Elaine that he got a court order to prevent her from trying to see him. He feared she would try to force herself into his presence—so he got out an injunction, or something, to keep her from coming near him. That turned into something of a boomerang.

John owed sixty-eight thousand dollars; he was that much in debt. He went to court and fixed up some kind of deal, and that was all right—until the judge announced that Elaine would have to be there to sign the documents. Legally Barrymore's wife, she would have to be in the party consummating the settlement. But how could she—when there was a court order forbidding her to enter the presence of John? One court forbade it, another demanded it—and it was worth sixty-eight thousand dollars to Barrymore. All of which surely was enough to wrinkle the brow of the Great Profile—until the legal snare was untangled.

In his later years, the poet D'Annunzio was haunted by the thought of death, as in his earlier years he seemed mad with the lust of life. The young poet who set Italy aflame with his incredibly brilliant poems, novels and plays, master of the flaming and sensuous style. The flagrant lover whose affairs made scandal around the world. The genius adored by Duse, who devoted her dazzling career and topmost fame to him, and whom he betrayed with a book that destroyed her —a book that was a prodigy of literary genius. The warrior who flung himself into the conflict of the nations, flew and fought as an aviator. The international adventurer who with his own private army seized the city of Fiume, in defiance of the Versailles Peace Conference. Picture of a genius maddened by life—that small, incredible, bald, egg-headed, ugly man, who was the darling of gods and women.

In later years, his "life madness" turned into a fantasy of death. A world poet, idol of Italy, he lived in a fabulous villa, in which he created for himself a strange room. He called it his "dying room." It was decorated with daggers, pistols and bombs—instruments of death.

In Italy I heard fantastic stories of how once a year D'Annunzio would create a fiction for a day—that he was dead. On that day he would retire to his dying room, and consider himself no longer in the land of the living. I was told that his early day of death was the anniversary of the day when a woman pushed D'Annunzio off a balcony. He landed on his head, and nearly died.

He always said he wanted to be buried amid the surroundings of his dying room, the daggers, pistols and bombs. He wanted to be wrapped in a coverlet on which were inscribed secret signs—signs of which he only knew the meaning, signs of death. His last book was published in 1936, the final production of his genius. It bore the strange title, *A Hundred and a Hundred and a Hundred Pages from the Secret Book of D'Annunzio, Tempted to Die.*

What was the news about D'Annunzio on the day that evoked these reflections? He had died—in his death room.

That protean genius, George Bernard Shaw, was presented to the world several years ago in a new and astonishing guise—as a great lover—this in Shaw's very old age. In London the will of Mrs. Pat Campbell was made public. In it the celebrated British actress directed that a volume be printed, a book to be called, *The Love Letters of Bernard Shaw to Mrs. Patrick Campbell.* It was known, of course, that Shaw, the Irish master of mordant wisdom and irony, wrote sentimental letters to the actress who starred in many of his plays. Some of them were published in the memories of Mrs. Patrick Campbell, written shortly before her death.

Here's an example of the Shavian unshaven romantic at his most fluent: "I hope you have lost your good looks," he wrote to the actress, "for while they last any fool can adore you, and the adoration of fools is bad for the soul. Give me a ruined complexion, a lost figure, sixteen chins, a farmyard of crow's feet, and an obvious wig. Then you'll see me come out strong."

So wrote George Bernard Shaw, and of course the Roman poet Catullus said much the same thing long ago.

Let us now have an expression of admiration, a grand gesture of homage. Let us pay our respects to Monsieur Hippolyte Rosse of Paris. To be sure, Hippolyte went to jail. But mighty was Hippolyte! What a businessman! What a lover!

It was not merely that he organized a stock company for big-game shooting in Africa—although that in itself was a stroke of genius. Hippolyte's plan was to stock an African reservation with hordes of lion, rhinoceros, giraffe and water buffalo. Impregnable shelters, wild-animal-proof, almost bomb-proof, were to be constructed, from which the shooting was to be done. The stockholders in Hippolyte's company were to have the right to blaze away at the game, and were given a guarantee that they would be so safe in the shelters that not all the wild beasts in Africa could lay a tooth or a claw on them. Many Frenchmen bought shares in Hippolyte's big-game-shooting company.

But that bright idea was dull and opaque beside Hippolyte's more scintillating vision. What would they do with all those lions after they'd shot them? "Voilà, Monsieur! Is there not such a thing as a canning industry? Do they not put up sardines in tins? Why not lions?" Very well, they would have canned lion steaks. So Hippolyte started another company—International Canned Lion Steaks, Incorporated. And he sold shares. His sales talk painted unlimited possibilities. Lions' meat would make a man strong, would make a man a lion. What Frenchman would not yearn to be a lion? What Frenchwoman would not want to be the sweetheart of a lionlike man? You see, the sales of canned Leo would be enormous.

But even these grandeurs are not the highest reason why I call for homage to Hippolyte. He not only had the gift of salesmanship, but also a gift with the ladies. The king of canned lion meat was young, tall and stately, with a flowing blond beard. He looked like a viking. When he addressed a lady she thought that she'd been eating some of his canned lion meat. So it was that he achieved a remarkable exploit of salesmanship.

He took another fellow's girl. She was a lovely mademoiselle. She left the other fellow for Hippolyte. Hippolyte sold her a lot of shares in International Canned Lion Steaks, Incorporated. That was not so incredible, ladies being sentimental. But Hippolyte went to the discarded lover and apologized. He explained to the woe-begone suitor how such matters of the heart were beyond human control. He was so persuasive that the discarded lover not only forgave him but became his good friend. And Hippolyte sold him a lot of shares in the canned lion meat industry. So no wonder I say, "Hats off to Hippolyte!"

He was swaggering around Paris with an income of twenty-five thousand dollars a year, a magnificent boulevardier—when the gendarmes stepped in. They said in their coarse way that he was a swindler. He was put on trial. But even in this melancholy juncture Hippolyte's spirit was not cast down. While he was under accusation he started promoting a new scientific way to determine the sex of unborn babies. That was accomplished by means of a white medicine. When the authorities analyzed the medicine they found it was plain water, water right out of the faucet.

The judge ended it all by saying—two years in jail.

Any radio performer will tell you that a sponsor is a wonderful thing. Here's a news story, however, which would indicate that a sponsor can be more wonderful than we of radio would ever suspect. In a New York court there was testimony concerning a forty-year-old man and a sixty-nine-year-old woman. For the forty-year-old man was on the witness stand and was asked how he had been able to get along for ten years without working.

"Well," he replied, "she sponsored me with gifts and

jewelry, and cash and property. Perhaps a hundred and fifty thousand dollars."

That certainly was being sponsored. The judge asked: "Why did she give you all this money?"

"Well," replied the witness, "I've been kind to her, and she has been kind to me. She sponsored me, judge, and I sponsored her."

So there was sponsoring all over the place—even more so than in radio.

Down Argentine way they have those romantic customs. You know, Señor, how they sing serenades beneath the lady's window—sentimental songs to the lovely señorita. Sometimes there is a serenade for a pair of newlyweds—that is so romantic. What could be more soulful than a party of friends singing ballads for a couple of honeymooners?

One night at Buenos Aires they sang ballads in such style that the police had to interfere. A huge crowd gathered before the house of the two that had just been married. The mob sang and cheered and made remarks. The bridegroom was Rodolfo Casco, a young fellow well known in Buenos Aires for his good looks—he was twenty-two, a perfect Adonis. The bride was Señorita Torres. The age of the señorita was seventy. In love's mysterious way, a romance blossomed between the twenty-two-year-old Beau Brummel of Buenos Aires and the aged señorita of the pampas.

That miracle of the heart produced a sensation down

romantic Argentine way. So half the town turned out to give them a salutation on their wedding night. The singing of love songs was so noisy and vociferous that the cops had to chase the crowd.

This is a story of Ivan the Terrible—or the Timid Bridegroom. Over in the kingdom of Yugoslavia, a young woman confided to a girl cousin that she was going to be married. But her bridegroom was so shy and timid that he wanted to keep it a secret. The girl cousin was curious. She watched and got a glimpse of the wedding party after the ceremony, and recognized the bridegroom as her own husband. He had married her in that same secret way—he was so shy and timid. That was only a small beginning. A total of fifty women came forward and claimed that same multiple husband as their own. He had been the bashful bridegroom of all of them.

Thus came to light the story of the most married man in the world. A traveling salesman? Sure—a Serbian traveling salesman named Ivan Torlesco. They called him Ivan the Terrible, breaker of women's hearts. They also called him the flying Don Juan, because he traveled from wife to wife by plane. He supported all fifty of them, though it was expensive. He had a time table worked out according to which he spent a week a year with each of them, explaining to each that his duties as a traveling salesman kept him away so much of the time.

They put him in jail, and he begged to stay there. He'd rather be sent to prison than face those fifty wives.

🐚

Here's a story about a bandit whom they called a Robin Hood. But he was a thief at heart.

The Robin Hood part of the story sang the Bulgarian praises of Docho Uzonoff, the Bulgarian bandit. Docho Uzonoff was a hero in the first World War, distinguished for bravery. But after peace was declared he was arrested on a political charge, accused of being revolutionary. Things looked bad for Docho, but he escaped and fled to the mountains.

The next thing you knew there was an epidemic of robberies. Docho had turned bandit. Time after time he made miraculous escapes from the police and soldiers. The peasants regarded him as a superman—a Robin Hood.

Docho never stole from the poor—no Robin Hood ever does. He robbed the rich and gave to the poor—that's Robin Hood for you. And they said that the plunder he looted was not for himself, but for the cause. He turned it over to the revolutionary organization he served.

But Docho, the Bulgarian Robin Hood, turned out to be just a thief, a burglar and a robber. He and his gang held up a motor bus. They took everything the passengers had. They packed up the loot and were about to decamp into the hills, when Docho noticed one of the passengers—a girl. She was crying, weeping bitterly. Docho went to her, and took her gently by the hand.

"Why are you crying, little one?" he asked in Bulgarian.

The grief-stricken girl replied that she was on her way to a neighboring town to be married, and Docho's men had stolen her trousseau. And how, she sobbed, could she be married without her trousseau? Docho swore a loud Bulgarian oath. He, the Bulgarian Robin Hood—and something like this happened! He roared to his bandits and made them unpack the loot. Out came the girl's trousseau. Docho gallantly gave it back to the blushing bride-to-be, and handed her also a bag of money—to help her set up housekeeping.

Then this modern Robin Hood showed himself to be nothing but a thief at heart—because he stole a kiss.

King Kong was dead—the King Kong of Harlem—that huge black giant who was the admiration, the terror and the great lover of New York's Negro colony. In a local police station a tiny brown woman told how she did it: "Yah, I done it. I done it with a butcher knife. He wa'n't no good." It was a story of dark tragedy in dark Harlem.

His real name was Willy Smith, but nobody called him that. He was six foot eight in stature, and had fists the size of footballs. Once he got into an argument with fifteen longshoremen, and beat them to a frazzle.

Whenever he started raising ructions and the cops came, it was always a riot call—at least four burly Harlem policemen to handle him. Would you call a man like that Willy Smith? No! Harlem called him King Kong.

He had a taste for strong liquors. He quaffed the flowing bowl of Harlem gin. When he did, he was all right. When King Kong was sober he was a terror, but when he was drunk he was gentle and mild. If he took enough gin a harsh word from a man half his size would make him speak softly, apologetically; he would be hurt, would even weep.

He met Mary Williams from North Carolina, less than half his weight. King Kong honored her by allowing her to walk beside him down Lenox Avenue. When he was drunk he was her affectionate loving man, but when he was sober, woe betide Mary Williams from North Carolina!

Now comes black catastrophe. King Kong met Mary Williams on Lenox Avenue. He was sober. She knew it. She smelled his breath. He growled: "Come along with me." She said, "No." She was afraid of him when he was sober. King Kong just picked her up, tucked her under one arm, and in sober fury carried her up to his Harlem flat.

He was sober once too often. An hour later Mary Williams of North Carolina was in the police station telling how she did it—with a butcher knife. That man King Kong never was no good when he was sober.

A bringer of glad tidings landed on our shores—glad tidings for lonesome ladies who yearned for companionship and had the price to pay for it. Ted Peckham was an enterprising impresario who made a business of providing dining and dancing escorts for women who otherwise would dine alone—and perhaps dance alone. I suppose you might say gigolos, though Ted achieved his climax by hiring British lords, noblemen of high degree. It might be lacking in respect for the British peerage to say, "His Lordship, the Gigolo."

Ted Peckham told how in London he lined up six English noblemen to come to America for hire as professional escorts. They were genuine peers with eighteen-carat coronets, the real McCoy, as Ted stated. How did he get them? What was his social entrée? He advertised in the London papers, put in a want ad for lords. And he got them.

Here's how he named them: Lord Howard of Effingham, of the same name as Queen Elizabeth's admiral who fought the Spanish armada; Lord Kinnoull, Premier Earl of Scotland; also Lords Townsend, Selby, Massy, Hindlip and Montague—all in Burke's Peerage. Booked to play the squire to lonely ladies in New York—for a fee. They were also said to be engaged to appear in a New York show to be called "Gentlemen for Hire." They'd combine their stage appearance with the duties of professional escortship. That was the story —a dazzling social vision for women who lacked companionship and did not lack the price.

However, the word from London was not so rosy. A statement was issued by Lord Kinnoull, on the Ted

Peckham list as Premier Earl of Scotland. His Lordship admitted that he answered Ted's advertisement, answered it in company with Lord Berners. But he said he did it to protest against the insult to British aristocracy. The nobleman expressed himself in these words: "It is deucedly impertinent that American showmen think they can come over here and buy peers like they can cigarettes."

Lord Berners added that in answering the advertisement, he suggested to the American impresario that he —His Lordship—would do a strip tease. Now that was something to delight the soul of a Broadway showman —a peer of the realm practicing the Minsky art of disrobing to music. What did Ted Peckham think of it? "He took me quite seriously," declared Lord Berners. "He said he thought it could be managed." Fancy that!

XII

Cracked Wedding Bells

Since marriage is the conventional goal of love, it were well to examine the story record of holy wedlock. What we find might be discouraging, save for the reflection that marriage exemplifies excellently the venerable adage about no news being good news. When connubial bliss goes smoothly, there are few stories either for the neighbors to gossip about or for the newspapers to print. On the other hand, a thumping family row is perfection for gossip or a news quip.

The Frenchman with the most troubled married life was dead, and in the sweet-smelling world of perfume the flag flew at half-mast. François Coty, king of lilac and jasmine, fragrant emperor of soulful smells, was gone from this world of flowers. His married life had been something fierce. Never before had there been so much domestic unhappiness so flamboyantly advertised. Yet it had begun with charming romance. Even the sourest marriage may begin sweetly.

François Coty was a red-headed young man from Corsica. He claimed some sort of kinship with that other Corsican, Napoleon. There was a certain similarity between them. Napoleon was the emperor of gunpowder and pitched battles. François Coty was an emperor of rose fragrance and domestic battles. When he came from Corsica he hadn't a sou—not even a centime. He loved a girl equally poor. They were like turtle-doves. Her brother lent them enough money to get married. The blissful young couple started a little perfume shop. Madame mixed the essences. Monsieur went around drumming up business. They worked, they struggled, they were happy.

It was François Coty who brought a new and inspired principle into the business of pleasing the nose. He introduced psychology into perfumes, made them romantic, alluring, mysterious. He began those names of swooning ecstasy—like "Seduction of Night," "Your Sin," "Tonight" and "At Once." A fancy name seemed to make perfume smell better and sell better, and François Coty climbed dizzily to the topmost pinnacle of sweet-scented prosperity.

His millions were fabulous—as many million francs as would make two hundred and fifty million dollars.

He went in for magnificent estates, and bought the
hunting pavilion of Madame Du Barry, the king's
lady, so powerful, so frail. He also went in for newspapers. He owned ten of the most important, including
the powerful Paris *Le Figaro.* He got himself elected to
the French Senate, but was thrown out on charges of
corruption. His election didn't smell so sweet. But he
was in every respect the grand master of the human
nose, lord of the sense of smell. But when perfumed
triumph walked in the palatial door, love flew out of
the equally palatial window. The king and queen of
flowery odors started one of the greatest domestic battles in the history of that eternal warfare. It was the
talk of France, of the French newspapers and the
French courts.

Monsieur Coty had a great advantage in the newspapers he owned. He used them mightily in his battle
with Madame. Often enough all important foreign and
domestic news—declarations of war and the fall of the
Cabinet—was shoved off the front pages just to make
way for Monsieur's accusations against Madame. The
king of sweet perfumes spread sour-smelling charges
in the biggest of headlines.

Not having any newspapers, Madame for a long time
couldn't make a public reply. But then that was reme-
died. After long and violent proceedings, the courts
granted her twenty million dollars in alimony, including *Le Figaro,* the most important of the Coty newspapers. Then she printed her side of the family row in
glaring type. The court decision brought the whole
matter to a state of siege, with Madame trying to col-

lect as much as she could of the twenty million. She
never got it all, but she did get a lot.

The battles of the King and Queen of Perfume provided treasures of gossip in the cafés along the boule-
vards, with Parisian wits telling how the king had
flipped a handful of rose water in the queen's face,
whereupon the queen crowned him with a bucketful
of distilled lotus buds.

Mr. and Mrs. Hey of Bogota, New Jer-
sey, had a picnic party. Mr. Hey was a good deal older
than Mrs. Hey, who was a mere kittenish thirty-two.
They were picnicking at the edge of the Palisades, that
beetling cliff of romantic renown, when two men came
along, pulled out guns and hollered: "Hands up."
They then pushed Mr. Hey over the edge of the cliff.

The precipice there drops a sheer five hundred feet.
Mr. Hey would have been dashed to pieces at the bottom, save for his quickness in grabbing hold of some
shrub vegetation which grew on a slight rocky ledge,
a few feet below the edge. The two robbers threw
stones at him, trying to loosen his hold so that he
would fall. Just then a siren was heard, seemingly a
police siren but really an ambulance that happened by
chance to pass. The two men were frightened off; and
Mr. Hey, shouting "Hey, hey" for help, was pulled to
safety.

The next thing was a sleuthing Sherlock Holmes
angle. Ralph Dogwin, a young New Jersey state

trooper, figured as a detective master-mind, sniffing clues and making deductions. Investigating the hold-up, he noted the fact that October 30, the day of the picnic, was cold and shivery, an odd day for an outing. And then Mr. Hey stated a singular fact: that he had offered the hold-up men his money, but instead of taking it they pushed him off the Palisades.

The deductive trooper sleuthingly decided to ask a few questions of Mrs. Hey, and went to her house. As he approached the place, he noticed a big passenger bus drive by. It slowed up in front of Mrs. Hey's house, tooted its horn loudly, then picked up speed and drove on. That was the clue, a clue that many a detective might have missed. Trooper Dogwin inquired of neighbors, and was told that the same thing happened every day—a bus tooting its horn in front of Mrs. Hey's house. This seemed to hint of romantic sentiment, and from sentiment the trooper's thoughts drifted to insurance. He discovered that Mrs. Hey had taken out a ten-thousand-dollar insurance policy on her husband, without his knowledge.

The next task was to pick out the horn-tooter from among the drivers of the bus company. This done, the case was broken with abundant confessions. The bus driver and Mrs. Hey both told the story of how they planned to dispose of Mr. Hey. They hired two thugs to do the pushing. Mrs. Hey persuaded her husband to take her on the frosty October-day picnic, and led him to the edge of the most dangerous cliff of the Palisades.

The worthy folk of Bergen County were greatly astonished at this unfolding of evil in their midst, with no one more surprised than Mr. Hey—who hadn't suspected a thing until the police told him.

✤

We all know the tricks that some women can play—especially on their husbands. And this one should take a prize of some kind. At Worcester, Massachusetts, Mama didn't want Sonny Boy to become too chummy with Daddy. Why? I don't know. But here's what she did.

Daddy was Irish. Mama was French. Mama taught Sonny Boy as a little shaver how to talk—which is Mama's job. But this particular mama taught her Sonny Boy to talk French—no English, only French; and Daddy couldn't talk French. Instead of having Sonny Boy say, "yes," Mama made him say, "oui, oui." Instead of "please" she taught him to say, "s'il vous plait." So when Daddy would try to have a chat with Sonny Boy, Sonny would go parlez vous. So Daddy got a divorce from Mama.

✤

I want to step out right in defense of the name of Alex. It is a good name. There was Alexander the Great, both of ancient Macedon and of the National League, and then there was Alexander's Ragtime Band. So I don't blame Alex Nelson one bit.

Mrs. Nelson sued Alex for divorce in Cleveland on

the charge that he deserted her. Alex admitted that he did, but gave his reasons. He said that Mrs. Nelson went to the dog pound and got a mongrel pooch, a shaggy mutt, and named it after her husband. She baptized the dog Alex.

"Every once in a while," he testified, "she'd call, 'Alex, Alex,' and when I said, 'What?' she'd snap back, 'Oh, I don't mean you, I was calling the other animal.'"

And so Alex (the husband, not the dog) left home. The court granted Mrs. Nelson a divorce—but no alimony.

In Chicago a gentleman named Christenson was seeking a divorce. Part of his grievance against his wife was her peculiar way of playing pinochle. Mr. Christenson told the judge how his wife at one time bid three hundred and fifty with hearts trump. Said Christenson: "I led the ace of spades and she trumped it."

Now it so happened that the judge who heard the case was himself an expert pinochle player and he commented that this might be excellent play.

Whereupon the husband continued: "Yes, judge, but the next time I led spades she followed suit."

At which the judge was startled and exclaimed: "She couldn't do that."

To which the witness replied: "But she did. And when I objected she hit me over the head with the card table."

Mr. Christenson then went on to tell of the time

when Mrs. Christenson had taken up a coffee pot and——

The judge interrupted: "Stop! The pinochle incident was quite enough. Decree granted."

Every wife knows that a husband now and then can be just too mean and spiteful—anything to annoy and irritate the long-suffering wife. Take the case of the married life of Mr. and Mrs. Robert Vandermark of Rochester, New York. Mrs. Vandermark was granted an annulment of marriage, after telling the things that hubby did—"just to get her nervous."

He'd sit down and eat a piece of glass—and that made her nervous. He chewed up safety razor blades— which also made her nervous. When he started sewing on buttons—no, not on his shirt, on his skin—when he stitched a few buttons right on his epidermis, that was when wifie's nerves were just worn to a frazzle. She explained to the court that hubby was in the automobile agency business. Which didn't explain anything very much. But she added that he used to be a circus freak—and that explained a lot.

We all know what red-letter days are, those memorable days that you ring with red on the calendar. Take the case of a lady in Newark, New Jersey, who showed the judge a calendar for 1938, with a lot of days ringed with red as memorable

January 28—my husband blacked my eye.

March 13—he tripped me and tried to kick me through a window.

March 26—he knocked me into the bathtub.

June 12—he chased me with a hammer.

When she got that far on the red-letter calendar, the judge spoke up and awarded her a separation.

⁂

In a San Francisco court a lady socially prominent—an heiress, in fact—told how she and hubby had a quarrel. The argument transpired while wifie was in the bathtub. It ended in startling fashion, when hubby seized the heiress, lifted her out of the bathtub and carried her out of the front door, and left her there on the front porch. He went back into the house, locking the door behind him.

So there was wifie, locked out nude, dripping wet on the front stoop—shivering and so embarrassed. It isn't revealed what the neighbors said. The heiress, made a nudist in spite of herself, finally got back into the house by going around to the back door.

Apparently she never quite got over it. This was explained in court by her mother, who said that incidents like the bathtub outrage transformed her daughter "from a happy-go-lucky girl to a quiet, solemn little woman."

⁂

In San Francisco a couple had a quarrel. Wifie said she would jump out of the window, the happy home being on the second floor. Hubby let her have the last word, and walked out. He waited in the street below. Wifie was as good as her word. She climbed out of the window and jumped. But there was hubby waiting to catch her. He was a good catcher. Neither was injured.

❦

Every husband knows how a wife can lose her temper. In Hollywood, Linda Hayes lost hers. She was a movie actress, and in a divorce court admitted that she might have got mad at hubby a time or two—flaring up, angry, irritated. This began in the following fashion: "Once he dragged me across the bedroom by the hair," said she, "and that was the first time I lost my temper."

❦

In New York a husband was arrested on a charge that paid a mighty tribute to the heft and huskiness of his wife. Some ladies, you know, can at times display a disconcerting amount of brawn and muscle. The story was that Frank Mata, a little, puny sort of guy, got into a row with his wife. Many a husband will understand Frank's mental processes in coming to the conclusion that he did. He figured that the little woman needed a good licking. The trouble was that if he tried to administer it, he might get the licking. So he went to Frank Casta, a tall, broad-shouldered muscular giant, and hired him to do the chastising. It was a regular financial transaction, with hubby paying Casta a hundred dollars to give wifie a good shellacking, twenty dollars down and the other eighty to be paid when the job of wife-disciplining had been done.

Casta took the twenty, and then was bothered by chivalrous instincts. He reminded himself that no gentleman ever beats a lady. His ethical conscience was disturbed. So what?

He went to the wife, and told her that he had been hired to whack her in sound, solitary fashion, but said that he would refrain from doing so if she would cooperate. He explained that he wanted her to put on some bandages and convince her husband that she had got a good walloping, so that Casta could collect the eighty dollars that still remained to be paid. That would enable him to gratify his chivalrous instincts by not giving her the beating. Whereupon he departed, leaving her to think it over.

The lady was indignant, as what lady wouldn't be under such circumstances? She was angry with her husband for paying somebody to give her a licking, and she was incensed at the intended woman-beater for trying to get her into an eighty-dollar swindle. She called the cops, and the interesting domestic situation resulted in arrest and prosecution. The legalities of the case were such that hubby was the one to face the legal music.

Just another painful instance of the old problem of what to do about women.

In a settlement on the African veldt, in the region of Johannesburg, a British magistrate sat in judgment over the complaints and difficulties of a variegated assortment of natives, white settlers and white drifters. Some of his most thorny legal problems concerned the marital affairs of the black tribesmen, domestic troubles in those wilds where the Bechuanas and Zulus range and roam.

Malapoa, a black man, was brought before the judge, and told his story. He married a girl and warned her not to talk too much. Malapoa didn't like chattering, scolding wives. Many times afterward he told her to be silent, innumerable times, over many years. Finally, on her ninety-fifth birthday, he told her she was talking too much. But she would not be silent. So Malapoa killed her.

The patriarch of the black tribes related this story with all the simplicity of the primitive soul. The magistrate could have had him hanged, but he didn't. "I don't know what to do with you, Malapoa," he said. "You are ninety-six, too old to be whipped, and too old for a long prison sentence. You have always been a good man, but you should have known it was wrong to kill your wife."

The judge compromised by giving Malapoa seven months in jail—and told him not to do it again.

A lady in Chicago went to court asking for a divorce. The judge wanted to know why, what had her husband done to her? Then she explained: "Your Honor, every time I talked my husband hit me."

The lady's name—and I assure you this is no gag—the lady's name was Mrs. Silence Golden Robinson.

In New York a man named Koprowski was brought before the judge, charged with trying to choke Mrs. Koprowski. The reason was, he didn't like his wife's jokes. The testimony related that Mrs. Koprowski had a great sense of humor, and liked nothing better than telling a funny story.

Mrs. Koprowski was such a comic that it was her habit to keep Mr. Koprowski awake at night, telling him jokes. She'd think of one while he was snoring, give him a good shake, and then proceed to tell the humorous wheeze—laughing and laughing as she came to the side-splitting point.

"And so," she testified, "he tried to choke me."

His Honor, Judge Ramsgate, sought to arrange a reconciliation. He turned to Mr. Koprowski and explained that jokes and humor have their place in the world—and help to make life a little less grim.

To which Mr. Koprowski merely replied, "I don't like jokes."

"Aren't your wife's jokes any good?" His Honor persisted.

219

Mrs. Koprowski interrupted. "Sure they are good—they're just so funny," and she laughed heartily.

"Her jokes are no good," said Mr. Koprowski.

The magistrate decided that he'd pass judgment on that point, and so he asked Mrs. Koprowski to tell one of her side-splitters. She was only too willing. Mrs. Koprowski, as you may surmise from her name, was Polish, and she could tell her jokes only in Polish. So she rattled one off in that melodious language, laughing hilariously as she related it. The judge didn't understand Polish—so he laughed. Mr. Koprowski, however, understood Polish only too well. He didn't laugh at all. His face grew longer and more lugubrious as his wife reeled off her funny story.

The judge's verdict was a compromise. He told the Koprowskis to go home—enjoining Mr. Koprowski not to choke his wife again, and bidding Mrs. Koprowski not to bore him with any more jokes.

A famous musician sued his wife for divorce, and it was interesting to inspect the charge he made against her. The famous musician was Sir Thomas Beecham, conductor of the Seattle Symphony Orchestra, the eminent English maestro who made soulful the music of violin, trombone, bassoon and timpano—not forgetting the harp. Sir Thomas Beecham charged his wife with the following offense: "constant harping and adverse criticism."

I suppose the maestro didn't mind the criticism, but

the harping was altogether too musical. Maybe the famous conductor didn't like music. Anyway, the maestro's wife kept on harping, and maybe she did some trumpeting now and then, and perhaps she drummed it in, and then fiddled around, after horning in with a sharp or flat remark. All of which would snap the holy bonds, if not bands, of matrimony.

At Montreal a wife went to court asking for a legal separation. She was seventy-nine, her husband eighty-six.

The judge looked the old girl over and asked, "How long have you been married?"

"Sixty years," she replied.

Whereupon the justice expressed his surprise—why should she want a separation after being married for so long?

To which she responded: "Enough is enough."

In the town of Treviso in Italy a man named Bastianetto was drinking red wine in a tavern. At Treviso, in the Venetian province, the wines are excellent, and Bastianetto drank well and deeply; too well, too deeply. He became uproarious, shouting and brawling. He made such a rumpus that the carabinieri came, arrested him and haled him before the judge.

Bastianetto, sobering up, was a badly worried man.

"Please, judge," he begged, "please do not sentence me to pay a fine. Instead, I implore you, send me to jail."

"Why?" demanded the judge.

"My wife!" exclaimed Bastianetto, with a tragic expression.

His wife had a bad temper. She was always raising Cain with him for drinking too deeply of the red wine. So he was afraid to go home. Instead of paying a fine and returning to his hot-tempered spouse, he'd rather go to jail.

The compassionate judge granted his request, and sentenced him to a few days in the local lock-up. The police took Bastianetto to a cell, opened the door, and thrust him in. And what did he see? His wife!

She was there on a charge of intoxication. At home she had been drinking too well and deeply of the red wine, had raised a rumpus all over the place, and had been put in the Treviso hoosegow. So there were Signor and Signora Bastianetto serving their terms together in the same cell.

In an Atlantic City courtroom a large story of family troubles was told—a huge calamity of marriage, a copious case of a wife deserting her husband.

The husband, with the Italian name of De Parsio, was a widower with seventeen children. He married a bride with the equally Italian name of Calabrese—she a widow with eleven children. The wedding made a combined family of twenty-eight children—just one big happy family.

However, it didn't stay happy forever after. A few months later Mrs. De Parsio deserted her husband, and a wholesale desertion it was. She was thoughtful enough to take her eleven children with her. De Parsio described it in these words: "One night she and her eleven children loaded their furniture on a truck and headed for Philadelphia." Leaving him and his seventeen children.

The telling of this big family story was followed by a recommendation for a large divorce.

🐝

Over in England, William D. McCann, a miner, was separated from his wife. The couple couldn't get along. After a period of singleness and solitude McCann became lonely, so he thought he'd get himself another wife. So he advertised for one: "Young man regular work wishes to meet widow." He received a letter in reply to the ad, and after exchanging several letters of sighing and romantic rapture with the lady, he made an appointment to meet her.

He nearly fainted when he saw her. It was his wife, the same one from whom he had separated, and in her hand she had a document for him. It was a summons to appear in court on a charge of non-support.

When the grave and solemn British judge heard the

story of the sentimental miner and the sentimental advertisement, he burst out laughing.

"Good evening, Madame. I kiss your hand, Madame." This is a French domestic drama, and domestic affairs have a way of being flamboyant in France.

On the anniversary of her husband's death, Madame went to visit his grave. A party of friends accompanied her on her solemn pilgrimage. As Madame had married again, she took her second husband along. Presently, they were all standing before the tombstone, the men with their hats off—all save one. The second husband refused to take off his hat at the grave of the first husband.

Madame was shocked and horrified, and said so. Her friends were shocked and horrified, and they said so. But Monsieur, the second husband, still refused to take off his hat. In the fight that followed the second husband was badly battered. He was taken from the cemetery unconscious, and the doctors were afraid that Madame might soon have another grave to visit.

In the Philippine Islands Maximo Labrada lost his wife, and was so broken up by sorrow that his father-in-law said: "Let me take care of everything, arrange the funeral, and provide the monument." The bereaved husband agreed between sobs, and the wife's father went ahead.

The funeral was held and in due time the monument was put in place. When the grief-stricken Maximo saw it, he immediately rushed to a lawyer. In due time his lawsuit against the father-in-law came before the Manila courts. Because the inscription on the tombstone read: "Here lies Señora Labrada. She died of maltreatment by her husband."

❧

At Willoughby, Ohio, a man drove to a police station, and reported that his wife was missing. She had disappeared in a strange and unexplainable way. The man was Leonard Herzog, a Hollywood lawyer on a cross-country automobile tour with his wife and two children. They were driving along as usual. He was at the wheel, and turned to say something to his wife in the back seat. He saw the two children there, sound asleep—but no wife. What had happened to her? He was a badly worried attorney at law.

The police at Willoughby questioned him for clues, and the only inkling they could glean was the fact that Herzog had stopped briefly for gas at Rocky River, Ohio. That was forty miles back. They phoned to the Rocky River police. "Sure, she's here. Tell that guy he'd better come and get her right away. She's fit to be tied."

It turned out that when Lawyer Herzog stopped at Rocky River for a tankful of gas, Mrs. Herzog got out of the car. Hubby never noticed it, and drove off without her. He drove forty miles before he noticed that wifie wasn't there.

In Egypt there was a ninety-year-old martyr to matrimony, a venerable sheik. He admitted that he could pay alimony to the wife that had him arrested, but pointed out that he had been divorced twenty-one times and had twenty-one ex-wives. "If I pay this one," he told the judge, "the others will demand alimony too. It is the way of women, who do not understand the truth of the prophet, Allah is merciful! But I have not got enough money to pay all twenty-one of them, and so I would go to jail."

The venerable Mohammedan was in a tough fix. He had to go to jail for not paying one, but if he paid her, he would go to jail for not paying them all.

The divine phenomenon called love and the equally divine institution of marriage received some elucidation from a questionnaire sent out by the Alimony Reform League. The questionnaire made inquiry of two thousand women who were keeping their husbands locked up in the non-payment calaboose. Why did you send your husband to jail? Are you satisfied that he is in jail? How long would you like to have him remain in jail? Those were the questions asked.

They were answered in such fashion as to cause the Alimony Reform League to say that the alimony wives with husbands in jail were not merely illogical but psychopathic—suffering from a sort of persecution phobia. Positively sadistic! Most of them said they sent their husbands to jail because their husbands deserved it, although hanging would have been better. As to whether they were satisfied to have hubby in the coop? Delighted! How long did they want him to stay there? About a thousand years—or, as many of them elegantly explained it, "until he rots!"

One woman described her former lesser half thus: "He had the grace of a hippopotamus, the brain of a gnat, looked like a giraffe, stung like a wasp, and had the personality of a dead salmon." Which went to show her excellent judgment in picking him in the first place. But then, love is blind, and marriage has eyesight much too good.

XIII

Wife and Child

Family devotion is an affecting theme in many a story—husband and wife, parents and children. Sometimes there is infinite pathos, sometimes a twist of the grotesque, and sometimes family life is not so devoted.

In the New York Court of General Sessions, an eloquent appeal was made for a prisoner—a plea not by a lawyer but by a priest. He spoke in behalf of Ormond Westgate, a long-time fugitive from an Illinois penitentiary who for eighteen years had lived an upright life. A respected citizen, with wife and child.

Long ago Westgate had been convicted of robbery in Illinois, his second offense, and had been sentenced to a possible life term in prison. He served eight years, and then escaped—that was in 1924. Thereafter he lived the life so often pictured in stories, the life of a fugitive determined to go straight. In this his prison experience aided him. He had studied electrical work in jail. That knowledge he now applied, and became an electrician.

Sometimes things were hard, and he was tempted to steal again—but held back. He had battles with temptation, and the temptation ceased. He married. Later on, when he told his story, he said: "After I met Louise, all thoughts of committing crime left me absolutely."

He did not tell his wife of his prison past—not at first. It was not until their baby was born, eight years before his arrest, that he revealed to her that he was a fugitive convict. She advised him to go back to Illinois and try to clear himself, but he couldn't bring himself to take the chance. "If I had been alone," he later explained, "it would have made no difference. But I couldn't leave my wife and kid."

Westgate's long-hidden secret came to light when he applied for a job at an armament plant to support his sick wife. There, according to routine, his fingerprints were taken. These were checked and his identity was revealed—the escaped prisoner of long ago. He was arrested and hustled to the Tombs. Illinois began extradition proceedings, and the case came up in court.

In behalf of the fifty-year-old fugitive appeared the Reverend E. Harold Smith—the Westgates' pastor, who had married them. In a moving plea to the court, Father Smith testified to the excellent character of Mr. and Mrs. Westgate—good citizens and devout churchgoers. He implored the court to release the prisoner from the Tombs, and declared that he himself would be responsible for Westgate—until further proceedings.

The court acceded, and the fugitive who for eighteen years has lived an upright life, went home to his family. Later the extradition proceedings against him were dropped, and he was left with his family to live out his upright life.

It was the night of the Beaux Arts Ball, New York's big society affair. I'm not so good at reporting the social events of the blue-blood high and mighty. They don't seem so important. I'm better on items from the farm. But there's always fascination in contrast, the strange juxtaposition, side by side, of two things startlingly different. For example, there was another event staged in the same hotel where the haughty and snooty Beaux Arts Ball was being held. That other event was the presentation of a pathetic, tragic memento to Admiral Byrd. So let's look at the two affairs, with an eye to contrast.

In one case we see the grand ballroom of the Waldorf

flaming in a riot of fantastic color, the splendors of India and the gaudy sights of the circus. For the rich and the high-hat disported themselves with a combination of fabulous Hindustan and P. T. Barnum. There was a circus parade in that ballroom—Believe-It-or-Not Ripley opening the affair—and there was an exhibition of circus freaks and monstrosities.

Then the ball that followed exhibited high society turning into maharajahs and maharanees of India. Scores of social registrites togged in glittering turbans and nautch-girl costumes. They danced as imitations of the Akooned of Swat and the Begum of Bhopal. But I wonder how good the imitations were, how far even those bedecked millionaires were able to duplicate the encrusted masses of diamonds and accumulated treasures of rubies and pearls that gleam on the Maharanee of Seringapatam or the Maharajah of Patiala when there is an occasion of state. I doubt if there are enough jewels in the whole Social Register to match the knee-deep heaps in the vaults of the Nizam of Hyderabad.

But let's leave the wealthy and the proud to their gilded revelries and go on to that other affair held at the Waldorf, the presentation of the priceless memento to Admiral Byrd. Yes, more priceless in its way than all the jewels at the Beaux Arts Ball—than all the diamonds, rubies and pearls at the durbar of Hahri Singh, prince of India. Priceless, but not festive, joyful or gay. Dark and tragic instead.

At that party for Dick Byrd of the Antarctic, the inevitable subject was—Ellsworth. They talked about

Ellsworth, wondered about Ellsworth, still missing with his pilot on the vast silent ice of the Antarctic continent. What had happened to those two brave explorers, who days and days before took off in their plane to fly across the south polar wilderness? Did they actually reach their destination on the other side, as we all hoped? Was it merely that their radio was dead, silent, unable to communicate? A number of rescue ships were on their way to find out. Or were they forced down, lost in the frightful frozen desolation—lost forever in a modern ice age? Days later we learned that Ellsworth was safe, but meanwhile the dark questions were in mind when they made the presentation to Dick Byrd.

What was it? A memento of Scott, the tragic explorer Scott, who fought his way to the South Pole, only to find that Amundsen had got there first. Amundsen had beaten Scott in the race to discover the South Pole, the same Norwegian giant of exploration who later was to be lost in the Arctic rescue of the airship party of the Italian, Nobile.

It was bitter for Scott to learn on reaching the South Pole that he was not the first, but only the second. Then fate struck still harder. On the way back disaster overwhelmed the party—blizzards, ice storms. They couldn't struggle through—not all of them. Some got back, but others died. Scott himself perished on the ice, died in his tent within fifteen miles of the next deposit of supplies, not knowing he was near them.

The present given to Byrd was a letter written by Scott as he lay dying in his tent in the Antarctic. It was a page with writing in feeble, fading pencil strokes scrawled falteringly by a failing hand. In his last hour Scott wrote this letter to Sir Edgar Speyer, who was his broker. Lady Speyer, widow of Sir Edgar, now gave the letter to Admiral Byrd.

In it the dying Scott wrote: "We have been to the Pole, and we shall die like gentlemen." He thanked his generous backer. He praised the courage of his companions. And with failing pencil wrote the last thought: "I have my wife and child to think of. The wife is a very independent person, but the country ought not to let my boy want an education and a future."

Two things seen at the Waldorf: the pity of the tragic Scott in the bleak Antarctic, and the glowing frivolities of a circus parade and East Indian splendors at the Beaux Arts Ball.

From a mine disaster at Portage, Pennsylvania, came words tragic and pitiful. There was an aching pathos in every syllable from the coal-mine town, where rescue crews broke into the black pit. They forced their way into a living tomb, where a deadly explosion had occurred. The rescue crews wore gas masks, and those grotesque masks on their faces suggested the fearful story. In the deadly gas of the coal mine explosion all had perished, the sixty-three men who had been trapped.

The tragic and pitiful words were found on scraps

of paper, a series of notes written by one of the doomed coal miners. Which one? Nobody knew immediately. No signature, no indication. The only certainty was that, as the dread gas flowed slowly in, one of them, one of the sixty-three miners, scribbled a note. Then other notes at fifteen-minute intervals, as long as he could.

On one of the scraps of paper was written: "Little son—Junior, be good to Mother." Another note read: "To my Daughter—be a good Catholic." The last one, the final message: "I don't feel sick, but there's an awful rolling in my head."

At the stricken mining town in Pennsylvania, they compared handwriting and family circumstances to determine which of the tragic sixty-three wrote those messages, so simple and touching—and to whom they should be delivered.

Thirty-two hundred Hungarian miners tried to join their companions in a strange death strike at the bottom of a mine. They went on a sympathetic strike, abandoned their own work in other mines, and demanded that they be allowed to join the voluntarily entombed twelve hundred men and share in their doom of death by starvation, thirst and madness. Soldiers with bayonets and machine guns held them back, preventing them from thrusting their way into the entrance of the pit. And the wives and children of the self-condemned men sought, in tears and hysteria, to join in the strange underground act of self-torture, self-destruction.

A few of the men below weakened, and came to the surface. They were exhausted, raving, at the point of death. But the remainder persisted in their wild desperate resolve. Men sent down into the pit to negotiate were held by the suicide strikers.

This terrible drama began as a simple labor dispute over work and pay. The coal operators refused to meet the miners' demands, so the twelve hundred workmen descended to the bottom of the pit and telephoned to the surface that they were on a strike—a hunger strike. For three days they remained down in the depths without food or water. Still communicating with the surface by telephone, they sent distracted, crazed messages—saying they were hunger striking like Gandhi, saying they would never emerge alive until their demands were met. As time went on they raved, shouting and screaming, some going mad. But still they held stubbornly to their determination of lingering suicide. At times they threatened to cut off the air supply and bring upon themselves a much swifter doom—suffocation.

The authorities were placed in a perplexing quandary. They wanted to send soldiers into the pit to bring the strikers out. But the cage that made the long drop to the dim depths of the underground cavern would accommodate only sixteen. Only sixteen soldiers at a time could be lowered, sixteen against the twelve hundred maddened suicide strikers. It was apparent that the soldiers could be sent down safely only when hunger and thirst had reduced the strikers to helplessness. The authorities tried negotiations over the mine telephone, offered arbitration, offered concessions, but the death strikers refused everything—save a complete concession to their demands.

All the while a host of fellow miners and members of the entombed men's families tried hysterically to enter the mine, while soldiers held them back with knifelike bayonets and threatening machine guns.

The suicide strikers won out. At the last minute the Prime Minister of Hungary himself stepped in and spoke a few words to the mine owners. As a result, an agreement with the half-crazed men at the bottom of the pit was reached. Their financial demands were met to their full satisfaction. It was a matter of pitifully few dollars, for all that agonizing melodrama.

In Paris, Madame Germanine Davin was wealthy, elegant and accustomed to the ways of Parisian luxury. Her son got into a desperate scrape. He killed a man, an American living in Paris, and was sentenced for life to Devil's Island. He was sent shackled and despairing to that tropical inferno which the historic Dreyfus case made famous for all the world.

His mother did all she could to save him, but it was no use. Then blasé Paris received a shock to its jaded nerves—when the news leaked out that the mother, socially prominent as she was, had asked to be sent to Devil's Island herself. She wanted to spend the rest of her life beside her convict son in that hell hole of the tropics. The astonished authorities refused. How could Madame think of a woman of culture like herself condemning herself to exile in such a place?

She insisted. Time after time she had her attorneys renew her plea, and at last the authorities agreed— permitting the mother to share with her son that exile which was called worse than death. "If my boy has to serve out his sentence there until the end of his life, why, then I will share his sentence and live out the rest of my life with him," she said.

She bought a small farm on Devil's Island, and there she went to dwell. The authorities granted her a favor, a special privilege. This was the one touch of bright- ness, yet perhaps the deepest pathos of all. The convict son, in his convict uniform, was assigned to act as butler to his mother. Thus they would be for the rest of their lives, mistress and butler, mother and son.

In 1901 a three-year-old boy was placed in a famous English institution known as Dr. Bar- nardo's Home for Foundlings. For four years he was taken care of there. Then he was sent to Canada along with three hundred other children. Some of them be- came carpenters, masons, builders, engineers. The one we are speaking of went on the stage. He did well, so well that before long he was playing leads. Hollywood

237

sent for him, and there he did even better. His name when he was placed in that foundling home in London was Samuel Jones. Movie fans later knew him as Wallace Ford.

During the twenty years of his success on stage and screen he had one regret. He knew nothing about his parents. He sent over to England to make inquiries about his origin. The information he got made him believe that at least one of his parents was still alive. A letter from an aunt in Lancashire indicated that his mother was somewhere in England. Wallace Ford was determined to find his mother. The pursuit was as difficult as it was long. It finally led him to Northwich in the county of Cheshire. There, living in an automobile trailer beside the river, he found an aged woman. The wife of a blind matchseller, she was known throughout the neighborhood as "Old Mankit."

There was a Christmas meeting between the young movie star who drove up in a limousine and greeted the wife of the blind matchseller as "Mother." They talked for five hours, she going back into the dim reminiscences of her past, he trying to stimulate her memory with the few facts he knew of his own boyhood.

At the end of the five hours, Wallace Ford, the successful young celebrity of Hollywood, said of the blind matchdealer's wife: "Yes, she's my mother, I'm sure of it." Then he added: "I am happy indeed that it's all over. Mother has had a hard life, but at least she'll have no more hardships." He bought a house in Northwich where his mother and her husband, the blind matchseller, could spend the rest of their days in peace and ease.

✤

The following document was a United Press dispatch: "New York, January 3. Magistrate Anna Kross called a mother from among spectators in court today to take care of her wayward son—charged with throwing bottles through plate-glass windows. But when the mother, a demure-looking woman, stepped up to the bench, she was arrested on a charge considerably more serious than that against her son. She was accused of using a broken bottle to cut the throat of a woman neighbor. The woman neighbor was in the hospital for two weeks."

Quite a slice out of life, as the novelists used to say. The mother got into a row with her neighbor in a saloon. She picked up a beer bottle, broke off the bottom by striking it on a table—and went to work with the jagged edge. Hardly a mother to assume any lofty moral tone with her boy for throwing bottles through plate-glass windows.

✤

In a Brooklyn flat a husband, wife and six-year-old son were found lying on the floor. They were starving, had fallen unconscious from lack of food. Detectives searched the apartment, and underneath the mattress in the wife's bedroom they found bank books showing balances of four hundred dollars in her name. She had other money, too, a couple of thousand dollars.

Here was the woman's reply: "It's my money, my savings. It's up to my husband to support his family. If he's out of a job, so much the worse for him. He shan't touch the money I've saved."

XIV

Miscellanies of Marriage

Matrimony presents various angles, beyond the mere simplicity of getting along together or not getting along together. The diversity ranges from a ferocious massacre in New Guinea to the tale of the Michigan Lysistrata.

The campaign of the Michigan Lysistrata was in a state of collapse. Or at any rate, Lysistrata herself collapsed. She was Mrs. Clara Schindler of Detroit, who set out to end a strike in the Chrysler plants by emulating a classic comedy of more than two thousand years ago. In the howling farce that Aristophanes wrote, the women of Athens tried to stop the war with Sparta by staging a strike of wives—giving their husbands the cold shoulder treatment until they agreed to cease fighting. In the comedy it all ended when the wives themselves couldn't hold out any longer, and sneaked home to join their husbands. The story in Detroit had a different ending.

Fifty-five thousand workers were idle because of a contract dispute between the company and the automobile workers' union. And up rose Mrs. Clara Schindler, announcing herself to be the modern Lysistrata. She started organizing a strike of wives to compel the men folks to end the strike. She claimed she had ten thousand women lined up to emulate the Athenian ladies of old.

The Michigan Lysistrata herself was gray-haired and stout. Her brother and her son were Chrysler workers in the walk-out. Her husband was not. He had nothing to do with the labor trouble. So there would not have been much point in her joining the marital cold-shoulder campaign.

The collapse of the modern Lysistrata was explained by the fact that so many women came forward to support the frosty idea that she was overwhelmed with telephone calls and messages, and succumbed to the strain of answering them. So the strike of wives fizzled out—because of too much work for the Michigan Lysistrata.

At Chicago an attempted hold-up turned into a comedy of life in wartime—with accent on the woman who works in war industry.

Walter Holberg, mild and middle-aged, walked into a shop dealing in gold and precious gems, and announced: "This is a hold-up!" And, with that, he pulled from under his coat two toy pistols, and pointed them at the jeweler.

The jeweler just walked outside and called the cops. When they arrived the robber said gratefully, "Okay, I wanted to be pinched."

In court Walter Holberg explained it all by saying that his wife worked in a defense plant and left him home to look after the house. The usual rôles reversed —the wife hurrying off to her job every morning, with the husband left to do the housework and take care of the baby.

"I have to stay home and cook, wash, iron and sweep and all that stuff," he said, and added, "I thought I'd prefer jail."

The judge reminded the prisoner that the sentence for attempted robbery could be as high as fourteen years in prison. That made the houseworking husband blink, and exclaim: "Your Honor, I've changed my mind, I'd like to get back to my dusting. The house must be a fright, and I don't think washing dishes is so bad after all."

He said he would much rather get housemaid's knee than prison-cell lumbago.

The judge dismissed the case and the latest report was that wifie, working at her war industry job, decided that hubby wouldn't have to do so much of the house-work thereafter. She would even get a maid to take care of the baby.

In Uganda, in Africa, a code was put into effect. A most important code over there, or else-where, concerning brides. Formerly there used to be endless haggling between the would-be bridegroom and the father of the would-be bride. Papa naturally wanted to get as much as he could for his daughter, while son-in-law didn't want to pay any more than he had to. There was a lot of dispute about unethical practices. Fathers with a large supply of daughters on hand would cut prices and bring about a condition of ruinous competition. Hence a code was established, with five head of cattle as the price per bride.

A perplexing case was that of a young man who said that the loved one he had his eye on was not worth five cows. The young lady's father, however, held out for the code price. During a public hearing by the British administrator, it was established that the bride was neither lame, halt nor blind. So Papa won. Then, after a few months of marriage, the husband appealed, saying that the lady had not been worth five cows. He wanted his money back, or rather his cattle back, all five of them.

Evidently that was a tough case, for the trial lasted for two days. The decision on the subject was worthy of Solomon. The divorce was granted and the bride, now second-hand, was returned to her father. He was instructed to give back three of the five cows and keep two of them. However, if the daughter developed a re-sale value, if another warrior came along who was willing to pay more than three cows, the ex-husband was to receive the surplus. The calves, if any, were to be divided equally.

Here is something for the woman's page —a wild massacre amid the dark and barbarous forest haunts of the island of New Guinea. It emphasizes Kipling's theory about the deadliness of the female of the species as compared with the male.

There were two tribes chronically on the warpath, but they had made peace and everything was quiet and friendly. The warriors of one tribe paid a visit to the warriors of the other. It was entirely a business visit, for the purpose of trade. The men of the two tribes gathered in a circle, and spoke friendly words. They exchanged tobacco and started smoking. It was a New Guinea pipe-of-peace affair. Then they bartered, trad-ing corn, yams, the skins of animals, glass beads and what not. It was a long-drawn-out affair, with the for-mer enemies becoming more and more friendly all the time.

From a distance the women of the home tribe looked on. Heaven knows what they thought or felt, but pres-ently they had a plan of their own. The next thing the warriors knew there was a shrill uproar, a wild chant and a stamping of feet. They saw the women approaching in a procession. They were dancing. They broke into the circle of the warriors, droning a weird song and moving in the steps of a grotesque dance.

The peoples of those South Seas, like most primitive tribes, spend a good deal of their time dancing. They have dances for every occasion. One frequent feature is a sacred dance for the women, which may symbolize a marriage, or may be a war dance, with the women calling upon their husbands to fight.

So it was that into that peace meeting of New Guinea warriors the women of the home tribe burst, dancing the war dance. They paraded before their men, stamping and shrieking in wilder and wilder frenzy. In the old traditional way they called upon the men to deserve their women by performing savage deeds.

The men of the tribe watched and listened in growing excitement. The visitors were aghast. Then, at the frightful climax of the dance, the women thrust war clubs and war hatchets into the hands of their men, and the infuriated dancers seized the visiting tribesmen by the hair and held them. Five of the visitors were lucky enough to break away and dart into the jungles. The rest, seventeen in all, were killed.

The peace meeting that went wrong ended in another dance, as the warriors and their women flung themselves into the mad gyrations that accompany the return of the fighters from battle and signalize the welcome that the women give.

At Aberdeen, South Dakota, Virgil Schense became his father's brother-in-law and the uncle of his three brothers and sisters. His three sisters became nieces of his wife and also her sisters-in-law. His wife became her sister's daughter-in-law and her father-in-law's sister-in-law and also her husband's aunt.

Now how did things get that way? In case you can't figure it out, here's what happened. Virgil Schense, son of his father's first wife, married the sister of his father's second wife.

🌿

At New Philadelphia, Ohio, a double wedding was announced. A nineteen-year-old boy was to marry a sixteen-year-old girl. His seventeen-year-old sister was to wed the father of his bride.

I don't know if that confuses you as much as it does me, but the upshot of it would be that the sister would become her brother's mother-in-law, and the brother of the sister would become his father-in-law's brother-in-law. And his bride would become her father's sister-in-law. And their children would be first cousins of the sister-in-law's mother-in-law.

🌿

How's your kin-mother? That's what she should be called, according to a pronunciamento issued in New York. Your kin-mother is the lady whose daughter is your wife, or the lady whose son is your husband. Briefly, your mother-in-law—although that ancient name was now tossed formally into the discard.

The New York Mother-in-Law Association considered the disfavor in which the name of "mother-in-law" was held. What to do about it? How to restore the name "mother-in-law" to favor. The Association shook its collective head sadly. The only thing to do was to abolish the name, "mother-in-law," and change it to something else.

A number of synonyms were suggested. It was proposed to call a mother-in-law a "mother-elect." No, you don't elect her, so that wouldn't do. Another suggestion was "happy mediator," which was just the contrary of "unhappy troublemaker." Still another was to adopt a German word and say "ersatz-mother." Another synonym suggested was the Teutonic appellation: "blitzkrieg mother."

The name finally selected was "kin-mother." It was adopted by acclamation, and in fact the Mother-in-Law Association proceeded to rebaptize itself. It was thereafter to be called the "Kin-Mother Association."

There was a weird wedding ceremony in India. The bride and groom were a couple of parrots. They were united by a formal ritual according to the strictest rites of the Brahmin religion. The marriage was preceded by a strange procession. The principal paraders were fifty parrots. Carried in their cages through the streets by their owners, they were accompanied by a band of music. The bridegroom wore a tiny crown on his head. A substantial dowry went with the bride. What a chatty household that would make!

❦

Couples were getting married in Puerto Rico by the wholesale, everywhere, as fast as they could get married. And all because of the difference between "caza" and "casar."

They had a radio broadcast in which it was announced over the ether waves that after June 10 all "caza" would be prohibited. Now "caza" sounds like "casar," and thousands of Puerto Ricans understood the warning to be that all "casar" would be prohibited.

Those two words may sound a good deal alike, but they mean very different things. "Caza" means hunting, while "casar" means marriage. So that Puerto Rican broadcast was understood to mean that after June 10 all weddings would be prohibited, and you couldn't get married any more in Puerto Rico.

That was why thousands of couples went rushing to the altar while there was still time. You can imagine the feelings of some when they found they had jumped hastily into matrimony, just because that radio news broadcaster got his tongue twisted and made "caza" sound like "casar."

❦

In the Caribbean, two men from a torpedoed ship were on a raft. For ten days they drifted on waters infested by sharks—and one of them decided to go back to his wife. That may have seemed rather an optimistic resolution for a castaway on a tropical ocean amid sharks. But apparently absence and the man-eating shark make the heart grow fonder.

Later, having been rescued, Sailor William Hoppe told how he went to sea to escape the little woman. "I joined the merchant marine at Mobile because I wanted to get away from friends who tried to get me fixed up with my old girl." In other words, he preferred the peril of U-boats and torpedoes to life with his old girl.

The fugitive husband sailed aboard a cargo ship and presently this was attacked by a U-boat and sunk. Sailor Hoppe and another man got off on a raft, and proceeded to drift for ten days.

"I had a lot of time to think out there," Hoppe related afterward, "and I figured I was probably wrong in the arguments with my wife. A fellow thinks of all the bad things he has done in his life and the good things he might have done, when he drifts for days and days on an open sea."

So there you have the picture—drifting on a shark-infested sea and repenting those domestic arguments. Of course, a cynic, cold and heartless, might say cruelly, the more the sailor saw of the sharks, the better he thought of his wife.

The fugitive husband, upon landing, announced: "I am going back to her."

To which we sentimentalists echo—absence and the man-eating shark make the heart grow fonder.

There seems to be something eloquently appropriate about a wedding in which the bride and bridegroom were handcuffed to each other. As they stood there before the minister to be hitched, one arm of the bridegroom was handcuffed to the adjoining arm of the bride.

It happened at Cambridge, Massachusetts, where Fernan Lowe was tipped off that some friends of his were up to a practical joke. They planned to abduct the bride at the wedding. But Fernan fooled them. He fixed it so they'd have to abduct him also. That's why the bride and bridegroom were handcuffed at the altar. They went off on their honeymoon still handcuffed together.

At Graham, North Carolina, Magistrate Charles W. Jones performed a marriage ceremony—a Negro couple united in the holy bonds. When the splicing had been duly accomplished, the dusky bridegroom asked the judge what the fee was—the price.

"Oh," responded His Honor. "Whatever you think it's worth."

The bridegroom dug into his pocket and solemnly handed the judge a quarter.

His Honor blinked once or twice. Then, just as solemnly, he dug into his own pocket and gave the colored bridegroom fifteen cents in change.

There was some discrepancy about the value of marriage. The bridegroom thought it was worth a quarter, but then bridegrooms have a way of taking a rosy view of such matters. The judge thought that marriage was worth a dime.

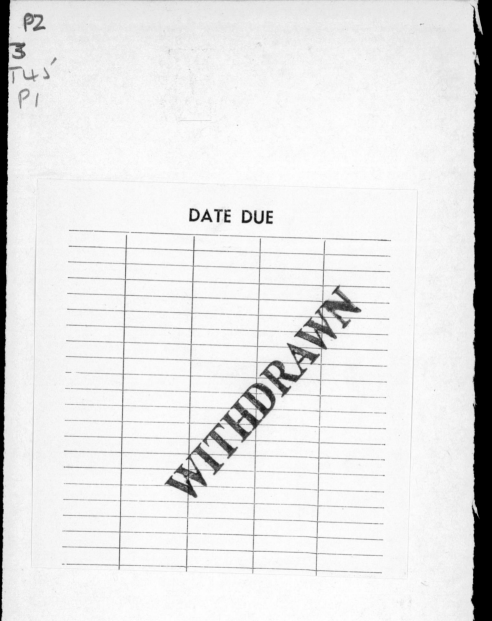

DATE DUE